W9-CHJ-123

BIG GAME, BIG COUNTRY

BIG GAME, BIG COUNTRY

by Dr. C. Guy Suits

*Great Northwest Publishing
and Distributing Co., Inc.
Anchorage, Alaska
1987*

Dedicated to Laura,
who held down the fort,
and wondered about
those bush pilots, while
I roamed the high peaks.

ACKNOWLEDGEMENTS

I am especially grateful to Charles Keim for repeatedly encouraging me to bring my notes to the light of day in the form of a manuscript. And to Jack Parker and Robert Stewart for the loan of some fine negatives. And to photographer Bob Burns for pulling some negatives out of very difficult sources.

INTRODUCTION

I have been hooked on hunting, and the tools of the trade, for as long as I can remember. I hunted very small game in northern Wisconsin as a boy, with a single shot Stevens 22 caliber rifle. Later, as a resident of New York I found the small game, and the somewhat larger game of the Adirondacks, and the Green Mountains of Vermont, equally fascinating. Jack Simplot of Boise, Idaho, and Frank Howard of Caspar, Wyoming, showed me where the elk, mule deer and Pronghorn antelope roam, and I loved every minute of it. That hunting brought into focus the importance of the ballistics of the hunting rifle — trajectory, loads, bullets, and collectively, long range performance, which has been a hobby ever since.

It was my close associate in General Electric — Jack Parker, past president of the Boone & Crockett Club — who first introduced me to Alaska and the Dall sheep, for which I am eternally grateful (Chapter 1). Before our first trip he set up a meeting with General Jimmy Doolittle, who had recently hunted the area of interest. After that meeting, I could hardly wait to get there!

Stalking the white sheep, Ovis dalli dalli, was a new and exciting experience, from which I have never fully recovered. Since then, no hunting has been in quite the same league. I am sure that my perspective is foreshortened, but for me sheep hunting is the ultimate. It is a game of skill, stamina and, especially, stalking. These animals can see about as well as we can with 5X binoculars. The Stone sheep of Northern British Columbia, Ovis dalli stonei, and the Rocky Mountain Bighorn, Ovis canadensis canadensis, of Alberta and the U.S. Rockies present equally exciting challenges. You may easily gain the impression that I am enthusiastic about the sport.

Jack Parker also introduced me to one of the great guides of Alaska, the late Hal Waugh, and his associate and successor, Earl Stevens. You can't have it any better than that!

It was my habit, which I can't explain, to keep a daily record of every hunt in a pocket notebook. That came in handy when Charles Keim asked me to contribute a chapter to his "Alaska Game Trails, with a Master Guide", published in honor of Hal Waugh. It was Keim's insistence that I write up additional hunts that led to the manuscript which follows. At the time I made the notes, this was the farthest thing from my mind.

If the readers gain some small part of the euphoria which I experienced in hunting the fascinating mountain top game of North America, I will be grateful. Good Hunting! CGS.

FOREWORD

THE ALASKA HUNTING SCENE
- A PERSPECTIVE

by Earl Stevens

Alaska was still a territory of the United States when I ventured there in March of 1948, as a homesteader, a fur trapper and later as a trophy guide, and I have never tired of its vast and magnificent wilderness. While guiding with the late Hal Waugh it was my pleasure to share many campfires and hunting experiences with the author. When Hal passed away in 1973 I acquired title to his facilities from Mrs. Julie Waugh and continued his operations. I retired in 1980.

Trophy hunting, and guiding, when Alaska was a territory was considerably different from today. The Department of the Interior, thru its Fish and Wildlife agency, closely supervised hunting and fishing, including the hunting guides. To obtain a registered guide license the applicant was required to meet many criteria, and to pass a lengthy examination. An assistant guide required no license. He generally served an apprenticeship under a registered guide, and then applied for a registered guide license.

To operate, a registered guide had to find a suitable unoccupied area to accommodate his hunters, and at that time it was no problem. Today it is almost impossible. At that time the hunter paid no special fees, and game was abundant all over the territory. Campsites in the bush were simple — tents, leantos, sleeping bags and a fireplace beside a stream prevailed, with an occasional Coleman gasoline cooking stove. Bathing facilities were nearby, in the icy stream. At more permanent camps, the next item was a cache, built over the trunks of 3 or 4 spruce trees, cut off at a height of 8 feet. The cache was the storage facility that repelled bears, wolverine, squirrels and mice. The actual repellents were the sections of tinned gasoline and food containers, wrapped around the spruce trunks. With a spruce pole ladder for access, almost anything could be safely stored in the cache.

It was common practice the carry supplies by back pack to the spike camps, some 10 miles or more distant, and to hunt that area at the rate of 15 or 20 miles up and down the local peaks every day, in search of a ram or, sometimes, a bear. Normally moose and caribou were hunted close to base camp, so that the meat, possibly many hundreds of pounds, could be back packed to the base camp cache.

Today, at the major camps, things are quite different. Small planes with oversize tires, and track and wheel vehicles transport hunters, crew and supplies to the various satellite camps, and return with meat and trophies. In some camps, horses are now used, in combination with the vehicles. It is against this background of changing times that the stories which follow should be viewed.

Post Lake, named after a member of the U.S. Geological Survey crew that mapped the area in 1918, reposes at the base of a mountain range overlooking an extensive valley bounded by the Post River on one side and the South Fork of the Kuskokwim on the other. Towering mountain peaks abound, some of which are snow covered year round. The lake is teeming with the arctic grayling, a trout-like fish which is delectable on the table. Post river, a tributary of the Kuskokwim, has the king salmon. The abundant wildlife includes moose, barren-ground caribou, Dall sheep, black and grizzly bears, wolf, wolverine, fox, mink, martin, snowshoe rabbit, beaver, spruce grouse, ptarmigan, gyrfalcon and the golden eagle. Anchorage lies about 180 miles to the southeast. The only access to Post Lake is by floatplane or seaplane. The only evidence of man's presence at the lake in the very early days, is the remains of a trapper's cabin on the west shore, and two caches on the opposite shore, built in the 1920's by Eli Metiokin of Kodiak, for Charley Madson, who occasionally operated here. Post was wild and primitive, and peace and solitude were its trademarks.

It was at Post Lake that Hal Waugh conducted the hunt for Jack Parker, Guy Suits and party in the 1950's. It was here that I first guided Guy Suits for Hal. Our only communication with the outside world was thru the pilot who would pick us up for the return trip. Guy proved to be an expert marksman, extremely accurate even at 300 yards. I enjoyed his conversation, for he usually had something interesting to talk about, and in an isolated hunting camp, that helps. Endowed with the spirit of the true outdoorsman, he delighted in nature, and its unique and inspiring displays, from breathtaking views from the mountain tops, to the colorful plants and exciting wildlife. In the pursuit of game, he was strictly fair chase. He has a skill, which I greatly appreciated, of magically appearing with some hot buttered rum at the end of a long and exhausing day in the field. Guy was a special breed of hunter and companion, which I found out on a total of four big game hunts with him in Alaska.

FOREWORD

by Jack S. Parker

I have been privileged to know Doctor Chauncey Guy Suits for thirty-five years, as a friend, as a hunting companion and as a business associate. I was delighted to learn that he had undertaken to chronicle some of his hunting adventures, for they are sure to bring pleasure to everyone who reads them.

Recognized as one of the world's leading scientists, Guy Suits has taken on every task he has met with consummate zeal and enthusiasm, whether it involved managing the General Electric Research & Development Center, or making furniture for his home, or photography, or flying an amphibious aircraft, or shooting a rifle. Hunting was no different. But in hunting, the days spent afield provided new surroundings, companionship and a relaxation interlude. I note that afield, he was devoted to *FAIR CHASE*, which I hold to be the single most important criteria for trophy hunting. This point is a major emphasis of the Boone and Crockett Club (with which I have been associated for some years) in the great role which this organization plays in North American trophy hunting.

Guy's first adventure into Alaska mountain hunting was with me. That hunt was a great experience, and the 21 days slipped away much too fast. Long before this hunt, Guy learned that I had been hand-loading for years, and he asked for guidance in starting his own work in this field. Soon the pupil became the master. Before much time had passed, he had acquired an extensive set of rifles of many calibers, and had brewed up a number of loads for each. His tests of rifle loads were very extensive and, predictably, outstanding. His first rifle range was set up on the frozen lake at his summer cottage in the Adirondacks of New York. He measured muzzle velocity, drop out to 500 yards, and bench rest accuracy for a great variety of bullets, ballistic coefficients and loads. Maximum gas pressure was measured for final loads. Measured results were plotted against calculated bullet trajectories. I still have a set of the curves he sent me.

The sport of hunting with a rifle in its best form is truly one of the great experiences of life. And when it takes place in some of the grand mountain settings of North America, it evokes memories that live forever. I am sure that this book will bring nostalgic thoughts to those who have had that experience, and understanding and anticipation to those who have not yet been there.

CONTENTS

CHAPTER I

DALL SHEEP OF THE ALASKA RANGE

The dall ram I had in the spotting scope was a beautiful specimen. His horns were a full curl, pale yellow and flared outward very widely and symmetrically. The tips came to a fine point, with no brooming. I could not count rings, but I estimated that he might be six or seven years old. If lucky, he might make it thru two or three more winters in the Alaska Range, where we were hunting. It was a fine trophy, but as I discussed the matter with Earl Stevens, my guide, there were a few problems. The first problem was that this was 1:00 p.m. on the first day of a 21 day hunt. Also, this was my first hunt in the Alaska Range, and I did not have a fix on the ram population here. Earl did, but he was hesitant to advise me, bearing in mind that we might not see a better ram — so, it was up to me. I passed up the ram, and it later turned out that this was the correct decision.

We were hunting in the Rainy Pass area of the Alaska Range, on one of the many unnamed peaks near the South Fork of the Kuskokwim. We had flown in two days previously to a base camp established by the late Hal Waugh, Earl Stevens, the late Park Munsey, Larry and Marian Keeler. The base camp was located at Post Lake on the west edge of a very broad valley bounded by the Post river to the west, and the south fork of the Kuskokwim to the east. The north and south boundaries were broad ranges of low mountains rising to about 5000 feet. The Hunters in the party were Jack Parker, Jim Suits and myself. Jack had hunted extensively in the U.S. Rockies, in British Columbia, and this was his third Alaska trip. Jim and I were relatively inexperienced hunters. But we were very experienced riflemen as we had used a lot of ammunition on my 400 yard rifle range for years. We had been handloading more than a dozen calibers, ranging from the .222 to the .300 Weatherby Magnum. We enjoyed the minutia of the ballistics art, and regularly tested the results on nearby woodchuck populations. We could explode chucks with a .257 Weatherby, and when our friendly farmers could stand for it, with the .300 Weatherby, at very great distances indeed. We both loved the .300 Weatherby, and each of us took a .300 to Alaska.

Jack Parker had used a variety of calibers on his many hunts, but he caught some of our enthusiasm for the .300 Weatherby, and used one on this hunt. We thus agreed on calibers, but not on loads. Jack regularly handloaded, but he was pressed for time, and used Norma ammunition loaded with 180 grain spire points. My Weatherby shot 150 grain Silvertips more accurately than anything else. I loaded them with 90 grains of #4831, and measured the muzzle velocity to be 3550 feet per second. The average three shot group, out of a cold barrel was five inches at 300 yards. Just to be sure, I had the H.P. White Laboratory check the velocity and pressure. They confirmed the velocity, and the pressure was 55,000 # per inches square (by the crusher method). Jim was convinced that 150 grains was too light, and he selected the 220 grain Hornaday round nose, at 2900 feet per second. It turned out that all of these loads were quite lethal out to at least 400 yards. There were, however, some interesting differences which I will mention later. The campfire debates about cartridges and bullets were terrific. Luckily, no one was stabbed. No one won the arguments. The last speaker had an advantage — he had the last word. But, unfortunately, a few ballistic questions remained unanswered.

I should have mentioned, that on the way up the mountain where we saw the ram, I shot a black bear. We hadn't intended to let anything divert us from sheep, but only a short distance out of the spike camp, established about seven miles from the base, Earl spotted the bear. A little arithmetic showed that Park, who was with us, could take the pelt back to base camp, flesh it out, and join us before dark. So, at 6:45 a.m. I shot the bear at a range of 275 yards. The bullet entered just back of the left shoulder where I had aimed, and was found under the skin at the far side. The pelt was black, glossy and in perfect condition.

After turning down the first ram, we looked over several somewhat distant bands of sheep, and then toward dark, returned to camp. En route, we saw a lone young caribou bull directly in our path. We did not need meat, but decided to have fun with this animal, one of the great clowns of the north country. As we approached to within about 75 yards, we remained under cover, and had no intention of shooting the animal, we only wanted to watch its antics. The young bull first reared up on his hind legs, and then, took off, with his characteristic prance, in overdrive, for distance parts. But in less than 50 yards, he had second thoughts (if caribou have thoughts), stopped, reared up several times, and stopped. He then decided that the whole idea was bad, and he slowly returned in our direction, with a gait that reminded me of Groucho Marx, and came within 75 yards. He went thru a good deal of rearing and prancing, and again took off for distant points. Indecision prevailed, however, and he came back again. He was nearly overcome by curiosity. He knew something was in our location, but we had his wind, and we didn't let him see more than the top of a cap. Earl said that if we had the time, we might, by waving a cap on a stick, bring him quite close. But we had the show, and had to get back to camp. When we emerged, he left for good.

HUNTERS STALKED BY SHEEP

Next morning we left camp late - 7:00 a.m., because of heavy rain, and we climbed to the area where we had seen many sheep the previous day. Although the weather cleared, by early afternoon we had seen no sheep. So, we found a fine high lookout, and sat down to have lunch. The valley we surveyed extended for about 15 miles to the south, on the west bank of the south fork of the Kuskokwim. Both sides had many steep rock slides, and the far center included a canyon which in turn enclosed a flood plain extending toward the south.

About half way thru our second sandwiches, a black bear emerged and began to work over some blueberry patches near an alder thicket. By the time I got to my Hershey bar, a band of sheep was spotted on the west side of the valley, about five miles to the south. While we were trying to sort them out in the spotting scope, they were enshrouded in a low lying cloud bank at the top of the slope. Before we had time to consider them further, we spotted two more bands, on the east side of the valley, about three miles away. Thus we had three bands of sheep where, a short time before, there were none. However, the sheep were not nearby, very rough country intervened, and the day was too far spent. But while we were feeling sorry for ourselves, a curious thing happened. The band of six sheep under the cloud bank, opposite, emerged running down the slope toward the bottom of the valley. They all seemed spooked. It is not likely that a grizzly was responsible, but we supposed that a timber wolf might have been the bad guy. Whatever the cause, the sheep continued down the basin at high speed, and disappeared into the canyon.

While we were discussing this strange, and very unusual behavior, one of the bands of sheep on the east slope of the basin also started to move toward the canyon, at first hesitant, but finally in full flight. We carefully scanned the slope they had occupied, without finding anything accountable for their behavior. These sheep also entered the canyon and were lost to view. Then a short time later, first one, then several sheep climbed out of the canyon, on our side of the valley. Moments later all 13 sheep from both bands had emerged, and began a slow ascent of the slope below us, grazing as they came. The impossible stalk we had considered 30 minutes earlier now had an entirely different complexion. The sheep were still about two miles from our position, but if they continued their present direction toward and below our position they could come within range. As the animals grazed up the slope they noticed the nearby black bear that was still working over the blueberries, and made a wide detour, also in our direction.

By now we could see their horns quite well in our spotting scope. There were four mature rams in the band, and two of them deserved a more careful inspection if a shorter range developed. We now became concerned about our position. We were perched on a rock slide with very scanty cover. The slide showed, we had noted much earlier, a number of sheep trails leading up from the bottom of the valley. We could be sitting in the local traffic lane, and we decided we would have to find cover. About 50 yards to the west of our position was a small patch of alders, so we very slowly made our way there, and awaited developments with great anticipation. Within the space of a mere hour this improbable course of events took place: The sheep, which had been beyond our reach in early afternoon, were now within 150 yards of our position. The sheep had, in effect, stalked us! As the sheep grazed within easy range, we examined the best heads in detail. The best head appeared to be identical with the one we had turned down the previous day, and for the same reasons, we decided not to take him. To complete the list of improbable events, a cloud strata which had been lowering all afternoon, now dropped a few wisps of fog between us and the sheep. And this was a wonderful opportunity to leave without spooking the sheep, so we grabbed our gear and departed.

On the way down the mountain to camp, we discussed new strategy. Although we had seen many sheep in this basin, there apparently were few mature rams, and we doubted that another day here would be productive. So, we decided to return to spike camp that evening and to base camp the next day for supplies. After replenishing our pantry we would set out to explore the broad range of mountains to the north. There were innumerable peaks and valleys in that area, and one of those peaks certainly would have the ram we were looking for.

As we descended the rock slide to the muskeg above our spike camp, Earl spotted a small band of five caribou. And since we would be returning to Base camp the following day and could not hunt sheep, Earl suggested that I shoot one of the caribou for camp meat. The small bull I took was shot from 150 yards; he went down without moving a step. While we dressed this bull caribou, his traveling companions behaved much like the comical young bull described earlier. They would all take off in one direction, stop, and again take off in another direction. They would then come to a sudden halt, and slowly approach us to within 150 yards, as their overpowering curiosity asserted itself. They finally left, but with no great conviction that that was the best thing to do.

The next day we got back to base camp before noon. Marian Keeler, returning for supplies, reported that

Hal and Jack had also taken a black bear, but no ram as yet, although many had been seen and stalked. Jim and Larry returned from their spike camp about 9:00 p.m. and reported that they had seen many bands of sheep, and, overall, more rams than ewes. Enroute to camp the two hunters had been unexpectedly delayed by two big bull moose, who were parked on the game trail they were following thru the spruce. The moose were expected to spook as they approached, but the animals glared at the boys, and declined to move off the trail. After some minutes of mutual belligerency, the young hunters concluded that it is very difficult to out-stare a moose. So, they took off their packs, and each located a climbable spruce. They then started to throw stones at the moose. This was resented by the bulls, for they probably had never seen people, and were curious. It took them about 20 minutes to decide to move off the trail.

WE EXPLORE THE NORTH RANGE

Jim and Larry's report of many rams to the north determined our course the following day. We left at sun-up and climbed hard until about 11:00 a.m., when we attained the summit immediately north of base camp. The area traversed had many steep rock slides, especially on the west side bordering the Post River. This was beautiful sheep country, with sheep trails visible on every rock slide. And as soon as we topped the summit ridge, we saw a band of eleven sheep on a steep meadow about four miles to the north.

The region was a huge basin ringed with rocky peaks. We saw the sheep on one of these peaks. Our spotting scope showed six rams, but at that distance the horns could not be rated. A direct route to the sheep was almost devoid of cover, so the only possible approach was a wide detour to the east, which we decided to take. By 3:00 p.m. we were on the side of the mountain opposite the sheep, and we began a climb which should have brought us to the point where they were last seen. But when we finally peered over a spur where the sheep were expected to be, they had vanished. By this time we had covered innumerable miles, none on the level, and in late afternoon were at least four hours from base camp by the most direct route. It was easy to conclude, at this point, that whoever wins a trophy ram, certainly earns it. Even Earl decided that he had had it for the day, so we started back to base camp.

We hadn't gone more than 200 yards down the mountain, however, when Earl spotted four rams on a meadow far below. The spotting scope showed that they were young rams, and while we were digesting that information, we saw six more rams on a ledge about one-half mile to our right, and somewhat above our return route. All of the rams in this group had mature heads, and two of them were exceptional. To get to them, we would have to cross a series of rock slides on which a fresh sheep trail could be seen. In spite of utmost care, some rocks clattered down as we traversed these slides. We finally came to a shoulder, where we expected to see the rams directly ahead. I took off my jacket and cap, and Earl and I slowly raised our heads over the ledge. There the rams were alright, but not where we expected them to be. The creatures were just disappearing over another shoulder about one and one-half miles away. Our trophy ram stock dropped several points.

However, we noticed that the rams were in single file, moving slowly, and obviously were not spooked. Also, they were directly in our return path. So, we decided to make one more try. There was a high saddle leading to the rams from our present position, so we took off at a dog trot and were soon following a fresh trail. When we got to the shoulder where the rams had last been seen, the footing was rock, so tracks were not visible, and neither were the sheep. Although we had a view that extended 180 degrees, there were no sheep in sight. Earl suggested that he take a detour to the right in search of the rams, and that I go to the left. So we parted, walking on a steep rock ledge with no sign of sheep tracks.

Within a few minutes, the route which I followed gave way to patches of shale, and on the first of these, the tracks of six sheep could be clearly seen. The tracks led to the top of a shale slide, and there disappeared again. I started down the slide, but found that the shale was at the angle of repose, and very prone to slide. So I chambered a cartridge, and sat down, then slowly inched down the slide on the seat of my pants. The slide extended downward about 300 yards where it ended in a small meadow. At this meadow, I now saw a small patch of white, which immediately disappeared. Evidently the slide led to an escarpment where the sheep were feeding, out of sight from above. As I watched, a rump, head, or a shoulder would show over the escarpment, and indicate where the rams were located. They appeared to be feeding to my left, where they were out of sight behind a rock ledge.

The full head of a very large ram showed occasionally, and momentarily, and I decided that his profile satisfied my requirements. So with my rifle at ready I watched carefully, and suddenly the big ram showed the upper half of his body. The range was only 200 yards, and I placed the crosshairs on his left shoulder and squeezed off a shot. Unfortunately, I had neglected to take account of the steep downhill angle of about 40 degrees, and the shot went over his back. But it couldn't have worked out better. At the shot, the big ram leaped first to the right, and then to the left, with the band following. Then, uncertain to the source of the shot, he mounted the escarpment, and posed full view, to reveal magnificently curled horns, with tips extending well above his eyes. This time I corrected for the 40 degrees and squeezed off a second shot. The ram went down in a heap, and never moved a step. As soon as I got down to the ram, I looked back up the slide where I had been, and where Earl and Park Munsey now appeared. That told the story. The sun was directly over their back, and in the strong glare, it was very difficult to see them. When I was standing in the same spot, the sheep had the same problem, trying to see me.

My ram's left curl measured 40 7/8 inches, while the right one was slightly broomed. We skinned it out, then took the head, cape and hind quarters and started for camp at about 6:00 p.m., where we arrived about 10:00 p.m. En route we had seen Jim and Larry high on a nearby peak, stalking a ram. When they returned to camp, they reported that they had high hopes for the old solitary ram. He was old all right, but careful examination revealed badly battered horns, so they passed him by. Park returned the next day to pick up the sheep's front quarters, but found that camp robbers, the scavengers of Alaska's high peaks, had pretty well demolished the carcass.

The next day we remained in camp to recover. Jim, Larry and Earl left early to find the rest of the band of six sheep we had broken up. Before we had left the area, Earl saw five of the sheep in single file climbing a steep slope on the side of the basin nearest camp. He said there was one more excellent head in the band, and felt quite sure he could find them again.

Our restful day in camp was very interesting. With the scope, some game was always in sight. A band of sheep spent the day in a high alp on a peak across the valley. Moose could be seen occasionally in the bogs, especially around sunset, and there were always many caribou throughout the valley. The caribou were still in the velvet, and no trophy size animals were seen. Hal claimed that he had never seen a really fine rack on a bull without a white collar. I agreed that a white collared bull was especially handsome, but we saw several bulls with immature racks and beautiful white collars, which raises some questions about his theory. The caribou's color/pattern varies greatly. Some animals have prominent black stripes running horizontally along their sides. Others have narrow black side stripes with light grayish area above, blending into a broad brown/black back.

Late afternoon I spotted a bear south of camp, in the valley at about two miles distance. I thought he was a fairly large black bear, and I interested Park in going down with me to take him. Before doing so however, we took a careful look with the spotting scope, and found that although he was quite black, his back showed the unmistakable hump of a grizzly. That killed the bear hunt, since the grizzly season did not open until the last week of our hunt. Later a large cow moose wandered quite close to camp, en route to the lake. I grabbed my camera and gun and started in that direction, having in mind some close-ups. However, an intervening creek prevented me from getting the position I needed, and fading daylight ended the mission. It was now 9:00 p.m. and Jim, Larry and Earl had not returned from their hunt. I presumed that they might have had a successful day, and crawled into my sleeping bag. I was awakened about 10:30 by a noisy return of the hunters. They had a great story to tell. They took a fine ram, and had a hunting experience they would never forget.

SOME THINGS A SHEEP DOESN'T NOTICE

The three had left camp in the morning and climbed the crest north of camp, bordering the Post River. They spotted several fairly distant bands of sheep, one of which they judged to be the five survivors from my hunt of the previous day. A long stalk brought the men within 250 yards of this band, where their scope showed an oldster with a fine head. Jim got set for a shot, but, as in my case, he did not allow enough for the steep downhill angle. He shot and missed completely. The rams scattered, but not very far. A bit later the old ram was located on an outcropping in the middle of a huge shale slide, which extended from near the summit ridge all the way down to and into the icy Post River.

After an extended stalk that included much belly crawling, the hunters were disposed around the ram as follows: Jim was at one side of the slide, back of a boulder, somewhat higher than the ram, at a range of about 175 yards; Larry was located higher up the slide, perhaps 300 yards from the ram; and Earl was at the top of the slide, in line with the ram, 600 yards distant. Jim was ready to shoot, but the ram was bedded down, chewing his cud, facing Jim directly. In this position, a shot was impossible, for a blood stain on the pelt of a ram, with straight hollow hair, cannot be removed, and ruins the trophy. There was no alternative position from which Jim could shoot, so everyone waited for the sheep to turn around in his bed. And this he was not inclined to do. So after about 30 minutes, Jim picked up a good size stone and tossed it on the slide, where it rolled down past the ram noisily. This did not interest the ram because sheep constantly cross slides with resultant clatter, and do not associate such noise with danger. Larry tossed some larger stones on the slide from his position, but with the same result. Then Earl tried some much larger stones. When these did not work, Earl finally found a large round boulder, and released it. There was a tremendous clatter of loose shale, the slide of which came close to the ram. At this point the ram decided something funny was going on, and he stood up. Jim's bullet immediately entered high on the ram's left shoulder, went thru his heart, and exited on the other side.

The mortally wounded ram took a few steps, and then toppled over before rolling down the slide and coming to rest far below. The ram was dressed out on the slide about an hour later, after which the hunters found it impossible to cross the slide. The slide was a one way street — down. There was no alternative but to descend to the Post River on the slide, all the way to the bottom where the slide went directly into the Post; as I found out a few days later, the water was only a few degrees above freezing. The Post flows very swiftly, and is about waist deep, so all equipment had to be carried high on the shoulders. All items survived except Earl's camera, which suffered partial immersion. After wading the icy Post for some time, the party was not exactly in fresh condition, so they had to cache their trophy and meat about a mile from camp, where they soon arrived, noisy but exhausted.

The next morning Earl, Larry and I went for the cache, and found everything in good condition. We carried it to the west side of Post Lake, where Larry had stowed a rubber boat. He carried the load back to camp, and Earl and I went hunting for targets of opportunity on the muskeg. The targets we found were the ones we expected to find, moose and caribou, and since we were not about to climb any mountains on that day, we went back to camp in plenty of time for a steak dinner. In my opinion, sheep steaks are in a class all by themselves, and Earl Stevens is a cook of very rare talents. With that combination in camp, one ought not be late for dinner.

I should mention that our "pantry" was now in great shape. We had one quarter of black bear, three quarters of young caribou, and six quarters of sheep meat hanging on meat racks, under muslin covers. All of this meat was excellent, and a preference might be difficult to justify. Mountain bears, in the fall, live on blueberries, and the meat is very flavorful. Caribou meat is fine textured, and excellent year round, except for the rut. Sheep meat is — words fail me — tops. Wild sheep bears no resemblance to lamb or mutton, but rather to a better grade of beef than you have ever had before.

Jim and I both had rams so we decided to fill out the rest of our trophy list. That meant bear or caribou, since we would not consider shooting a moose. Grizzly season was not yet open, so we decided to look for some black bears, which had not been too hard to find thus far. We took off in early morning for a high meadow on the foothills of the mountain range to the north, about two miles east of camp. The climb was moderate, and we were soon on a high bluff from which we could scan a tremendous area to the south. Jim spotted a grizzly on a grassy slope above us, at a distance of one-half mile. Since the season still was not open, we could only watch the bear work over the mountain side for marmots, which he was doing very effectively. The animal's pelt was dark chocolate brown, with a light tawny mane. We saw moose and caribou, still in velvet, in abundance, but no black bears, so we returned to camp in late afternoon.

It rained hard all night and was still raining the next morning. Alaskan weather is characterized by rain. Preparation for rain, in all items of equipment, is important on any Alaskan hunt. Typical rain gear keeps water out, but perspiration in. Hip boots with very light rubberized tops, and a waterproof poncho, is an alternative with some merit. The poncho permits air circulation, and the escape of moisture, and is better than a rubber jacket. I tried a set of rubberized chaps, over wool trousers with some success. Keeping the sleeping bag dry in a spike camp was a serious problem. In about three days, some bags will load with moisture, and fail to insulate. The only solution we found was

Base camp and Post Lake, Chapter 1

Two caches at Post Lake. Chapter 1.

Cessna 180 on floats at Post Lake. Chapter 1.

Looking south from base camp at Post Lake—Muskeg and South Range. Chapter 1.

Chaucey Guy Suits and caribou. Chapter 1.

Jim Suits on the east bank of the "Icy Post" River. Chapter 1.

Post Lake hunters and guide, top row, left to right: Jim Suits, Larry Keeler, Marion Keeler, Hal Waugh, Jack Parker; bottom row, left to right: Earl Stevens, Chauncey Guy Suits. Chapter 1.

Caribou at Post Lake. Chapter 1.

Rams captured by Jack Parker in his "Jack-pot in movies". Chapter 1.

Assistant guides with Dall sheep. Chapter 1.

Hal Waugh, a guide's guide, standing beneath his cache. Chapter 1.

Jack Parker's ram. Chapter 1.

The full house—family affair. Chapter 1.

Left to right: Jack Parker, Hal Waugh, and Jim Suits with full collection of trophies. Chapter 1.

Jack Parker's grizzley pelt and Hal Waugh. Chapter 1

Our Lake in the Clouds. Chapter 2.

to string a large sheet of plastic between tents, or trees and tents, and build a large fire, for drying bags. For this and other reasons, the spike camp should be below tree line. Nowadays there are excellent bags on the market, such as those insulated with Quallofil™, and these are warm even when damp.

Jack and Marion finally returned to base camp from the spike camp where they had been since the hunt's first day. They had hunted hard, and passed up many rams, but only had one black bear. So the two planned next to go into the area where we had found our rams.

WE CROSS THE ICY POST

We had been interested in some of the things we observed across the Post River. There had been many caribou, some with beautiful white manes, but still in velvet. We also saw a grizzly with striking coloration: the back was tawny blonde, and the sides dark chocolate brown. But, the problem was to cross the Post. The Post river consisted of a network of tributaries on a broad flood plain. By careful selection, a preferred route could be found. At best, however, the water was very swift, icy and a clear hazard. Keeping one's footing on the slippery rock bottom was the key problem. We decided to make a try on the following day. I had my fingers crossed.

It rained all night and into the morning. Jack and Hal left about 7:30, and their packers a bit later. Jim, Earl and I decided to ford the Post, and we left about 10:30, in moderating weather, which finally turned out to be a beautiful day. We had been watching the chocolate brown grizzly above camp, and if he was there on opening day I intended to put a 150 grain silvertip in his rib cage. This would give the marmots a much needed rest.

We were soon at the Post and facing our problem. Earl had hip boots, and was sure he could find a way across that would not go over his tops. A crossing involved at least ten branch streams in the interwoven network, and probably more. The tributary streams varied in width from 15 to perhaps 60 feet in width. We did entertain the speculative hope of finding a series of crossings with depths that did not exceed three feet, but it eluded us. Jim and I had decided, before coming to Post Lake, to avoid the weight and nuisance of hip boots, by an alternative. We would, and now did, strip to the waist and put on light tennis shoes. All of our gear was tied high on the pack board, and we started across the first tributary. For emergency use we each had a 50 foot length of 3/16 inch nylon line tied to our belt. The first four or five streams were crossed without problems, but as we approached the main stream, the increasing depth, swiftness and width left our legs white and numb from the cold.

Finally, we came to the widest and deepest tributary. Earl had previously crossed, so Jim took off. The stream was too wide at this point to cast the nylon lines across. Jim got two-thirds of the way across, and ran into trouble. The depth increased to four feet, with a very swift current, so that he could barely hold his footing, when standing still. Earl tried to get to Jim, but found that he could not hold his footing, and he returned to the bank. In desperation, Jim uncurled his nylon line and tried to throw it to Earl. With one hand holding the rifle out of the water, this turned out to be a problem, but on the fourth try Earl caught the line, and pulled Jim to the shore. Jim's legs were white with cold, and it took many minutes of rubbing to restore circulation. My turn came next, and with about the same sequence of events, I got across. At this point, I had some doubts that we had the best strategy for crossing Alaskan streams. But we had gone to all of this trouble because we had seen some very fine animals across the Post, in particular, some very impressive caribou.

Our hunt across the Post turned out to be a big ZERO. We saw no caribou worth shooting, nor any other game of interest. Late in the day we decided we did not want to be late for dinner, so we went back to cross the Post again. Independently, Jim and I had come to the same conclusion. We would cross the Post in our clothes, including our boots. Camp was only three-quarters of an hour from the Post, and in camp we could dry out at leisure. We did, and crossed without difficulty, and arrived at camp wet, but not frozen. We noted that the grizzly was still on the slope above camp, no doubt carefully watching the calendar for the start of his season.

After arriving in camp, we decided that we would take the next day out for game photography. We had in mind the vast muskeg area bounded by mountains on the north and south, with the South Fork of the Kuskokwim on the east and the Post on the west. The muskeg in the middle of this very large valley was a veritable game highway. Caribou could be seen at any hour of the day. Moose were generally in sight, but at sunset they were seen at many points. Less frequently, we saw wolves, black bears and grizzlies.

As we moved thru the spruce at the edge of the muskeg, we encountered four cow moose. Jim got his movie camera going, at about 150 yards, and slowly moved in their direction. The cow moose has the reputation of being evil tempered and unpredictable. So, as we approached, each of us kept his eye on a climbable tree. A cow moose is not beauty in nature, looking like she was assembled from spare parts left over from creation. Her face looks like a mule that has been badly fractured and poorly mended. Below the chin a cow moose carries an appendage of uncertain utility. With large humped shoulders, and deeply swayed backs, a cow moose can only be attractive to a bull moose, whose eyesight, in any case, is extremely poor.

After the moose moved off, we proceeded thru the muskeg and spotted quite a number of caribou, but none of interest. To gain a better view of the valley we found a knoll nearby, and on the way up I spotted a wolf at a range of about 500 yards. He began to lope off, and I considered what to do but finally came to grips with the fact that a moving target at that range was pure speculation. We watched him disappear into the spruce. Pity! We returned to camp late afternoon.

GRIZZLY SEASON OPENS

The next morning grizzly season finally opened, but a heavy ground fog prevented our departure for some time. When the fog lifted, we carefully scanned the slope where the grizzly had been feeding for about a week, but that day we couldn't find him. A bit later, however, in response to some concentrated spotting activity on the part of Earl, he found the grizzly. The beast was on the facing slope of the mountains to the

sight of the bear. By this time we were saturated with perspiration, so we sat down to wait awhile and see if the bear might come out of the million hiding places it had up there. In late morning, after the bear failed to show again, we returned to camp.

WE TRY A NEW SPIKE CAMP

Later Hal and Jack Parker returned from their spike camp. We then regained our packer, who had been with Hal for some time, so Jim, Earl and I decided to try a new spike camp — new to us — where Hal had seen abundant caribou, moose, black bear and two grizzlies. Bears, and a trophy style caribou were now on our want lists. I didn't think bears would be a problem, but, although we had seen very large numbers of caribou, a really fine head had escaped us. The animals were just starting to lose their velvet. While shedding, they can acquire a bedraggled look, but even that impediment would not fully hide a fine rack.

Personally, I had a problem with a really large caribou head. In the back of my mind I was considering just where I would mount it at home. I already had an elk that was occupying the best spot, and I was very fond of the elk. A solution is to build a game wing on the house, which Jack Parker later did. But I was not about to add a wing. Our Lake Room finally became a game room, and it is now very handsome with all its trophies. Caribous come in so many sizes and colors, that I felt a solution might be to find a small elegant head. These are very rare indeed. But on our way back to Anchorage we stopped at Bud Brannon's Rainy Pass Lodge, and there saw among his hunter's heads a perfect miniature caribou rack. This was not a young caribou — their racks do not qualify as trophies. This was a two-third size rack that was fully mature in its convolutions and structure. Most unusual were two fully developed brow palms. Hal estimated that this occurrence took place in about one in 10,000 animals. Some years later, I took such a caribou down on the Alaska peninsula. In any event, the miniature rack at Rainy Pass was a real gem.

Jim, Larry, Earl and I got into the new spike camp about 1:00 p.m. the next day, heavily loaded. One 7 feet by 7 feet tent, and a pup tent had been left there, and we brought one more pup tent with us. The location was a beautiful grove of spruce at the timber line. It was separated by a narrow strip of muskeg — our game highway — from the range of mountains to the south. We lacked only one thing, a creek. Our water supply had to be carried from a creek about 200 yards away. Thank God for packers! We made lunch, made things shipshape, and did a preliminary reconnaissance before dark.

The place was so beautiful that if we saw no game for a couple of days, I would not bleed. However, the game would help. Actually, caribou and moose were all over the place. Just beyond the camp area we ran into a young and very inquisitive caribou. On Larry's suggestion, we ducked into some alders, and he put his cap on a stick and wiggled it. The caribou couldn't resist. The animal had seen many strange things in its young life, but nothing like this! It pranced, and reared, and danced, and pranced, and finally came within 15 yards. The caribou tried to get our wind, but couldn't; there wasn't any. Even when we finally emerged, that did not spook the caribou. It merely moved off a bit further, and resumed its humorous behavior. When we returned to camp, two very large cow moose appeared, and came within 100 yards of our tents. We were not particularly fond of cow moose, so we stared them down, as best we could. It took them about 10 minutes to decide that we were not their kind of folks. Finally, the unlovely ladies left.

Earl and I left early the next morning, looking for a grizzly, while Jim and Larry went out for movies, movies of anything that moved. Our grizzly hunt was as successful as any grizzly hunt can be — without a grizzly. We had a lovely day on the lower slopes of the area. The blueberries were especially lush, and after an inspection of nearby areas, we found a nice soft spot at the upper edge of the muskeg, and sat down to scope the area. We saw everything but bear, so in late afternoon we returned to camp. Jim and Larry said they had some exceptional moose pictures. The animals had been very obliging. When we saw them much later, the pictures were very good, except toward the end of the sequence, where the camera was very unsteady. Jim explained that the moose became ornery, and started for them. That's when they climbed a spruce.

The next day had a bad beginning. At breakfast I picked up what I thought was a can of butter — all camp butter comes in cans — and found that the can had just been filled with hot bacon grease by Earl. I burned my hand slightly, but I dropped the can on my right foot, in stockings, not shoes, and received a painful burn. It soon became clear that I would not be hunting that day. Jim and Larry went up the slope to try for sheep movies, and Earl found a high lookout to scope the valley. I put some gauze and tape on my foot and limped around camp, wondering how long I would be on the disabled list. Later in the morning, I pulled my boot over the wound, and found that it was not too bad. I was only partially disabled. I walked up the slope Earl had taken, and when I found him he said he had not seen a bear, but he had a fairly interesting caribou in sight. We moved up the slope a bit, and then set up the scope for a more careful look. The caribou was grazing about 700 yards to the east, and in the scope it showed a gray/white mane, a long set of white neck whiskers, and beautiful antlers entirely out of the velvet. This animal was very close to specifications. We decided to climb up to within range, and if it still looked good, to take it. The caribou was moving slowly toward the gully which we had just ascended. We kept in alders and moved toward the animal. We came out of a gully and looked for the caribou, but he was nowhere in sight. We guessed that he was bedded down, so we started glassing the slope ahead in detail. In a few minutes I located a pair of antlers showing above some alders.

A light wind was blowing from our right, directly toward the antlers on our left. Earl went up the slope to our right, to give the animal his wind, which would undoubtedly bring him to his feet. I could then decide, from 150 yards if he was worth taking. I chambered a cartridge, released my safety, and took a good shooting position. As soon as Earl reached the agreed position, the bull arose exactly as predicted and stood like an insurance advertisement, trying to locate the strange smells. It turned its head from side to side, and posed for minutes on his high promontory. This was by far the finest bull we had seen, and would take care of my available wall area. So I squeezed off a shot, and it went down. The shot went thru the animal's heart, and lodged under the hide on the opposite side. We went up to the animal, took pictures, and dressed it out. When it began raining, we left for camp.

Shortly after we got back to camp. Jim and Larry returned from their photo trip. The rain and low clouds had washed out their expedition, but on their return, only 30 minutes earlier, they had passed a fine silver tip grizzly. He was so busy digging marmots, that he did not see them, and they got a fine movie sequence, from 125 yards. I was raring to go back up the mountain and find the grizzly, but I found no enthusiasm anywhere in camp. To add a grizzly to the work load was too much, particularly when I remembered that my foot limited my activity to limping and pulling triggers. So we had to give up this grizzly, much to my regret. The trouble with grizzlies is — they have no characteristic habitat. Sheep are on the tops, and caribou favor the steep meadows between the rocks and the muskeg, and moose will be in the bogs. But grizzlies are where you find them.

According to Alaska game regulations, as mentioned, all meat had to be brought out. The rule was designed to prevent wanton killing, and I approve of it. Accordingly, we had to pack our meat back to camp, and any meat left at the end of the hunt had to be flown back to Anchorage. We left for camp, and en route we saw, across the Post River, a sow and five black bear cubs.

Since our packers were fully engaged in transporting meat, Jim and I were anchored to main camp. That was not hard to take, for the sun came out and the day was balmy. Earl and Larry spent the day fleshing out the caribou hide, the end result of which was beautiful. When we left Anchorage, we were short one packer, and early in the hunt Park Munsey began feeling an illness which became progressively worse. We were now quite concerned about Park's condition, and Hal was considering the possibility of hiking to McGrath for help. Under forced draft, that would have taken two days, and our plane for the return trip to Anchorage would be here in four days. Our problem was solved when we were able to flag down a Fish and Wildlife Service plane which was flying over camp. He landed at the lake, and was able to take Park out, to our great relief, since Park was evidently in serious condition.

A JACKPOT, IN MOVIES

Jack Parker now had a fine ram, so he decided to unlimber his 16 mm Bolex and get some pictures. The first day out with camera he and Hal hit the jackpot. They set the camera up on the slope facing camp, on the south. After some pictures of the usual inhabitants of the muskeg — caribou and moose — they noticed a band of nine sheep high on a ridge across the valley to the north. They got a few pictures, with a 6 inch telephoto, and then noticed that the sheep were descending toward the tree line, and were entering the spruce. This in itself was very unusual, for sheep seldom go very low on the mountain, due to their vulnerability to the timber wolf. As the hunters continued photographing, the animals went down to the muskeg, and found a spot which immediately occupied all of their attention. It appeared to be a natural salt lick, and that was the lure which overpowered their instinctive caution. The animal's behavior at the salt lick was determined entirely by the butting order. The largest ram simply butted the lesser rams out of the way, and took first licks. When he was served, the next largest ram took his place, and so forth. Then a still more unusual thing happened. When the lick was over, the sheep, instead of returning to the north slope, continued across the muskeg and started an ascent toward Hal and Jack on the south slope. Jack continued to run the Bolex, and finally the sheep passed him on their way up the slope — within 100 yards. Jack got the whole sequence on film.

WE NEED BEARS, AND GET THEM

By now, my game list was doing well, but a grizzly was the principal missing trophy. In discussing this with Earl, we felt that, since there is no special place to go for grizzlies, our principal valley surrounding Post Lake was as good as any place we could select. On a good day the area available for scoping was very great indeed. So, we set out the next morning with this in mind. We headed for the NE area, where we found a good lookout on a ridge near the south fork of the Kuskokwim. Our day consisted primarily of searching with binoculars and spotting scopes. We had bands of sheep in sight during the entire day, and caribou were visible all over the valley. In late afternoon the moose emerged, and went to work for their evening meal. But we didn't see a single bear, black or brown.

We left for camp with the growing suspicion that our presence in the valley was pushing the bear out.

The effect of hunting is well known, and I have observed it many times since then. In discussing the matter with Hal that night, he agreed with our diagnosis, and suggested a valley across the Post, somewhat to the north, where no hunter had been in recent years. I didn't relish another river crossing, but time was running out, and we decided to try it.

We got to the Post River about 7:00 a.m. and were very pleased to find that the water level had receded a good deal from the high level that had given us such a painful experience earlier. I had borrowed a pair of hip boots from Hal, and we crossed without problems, then headed for "Bear Valley". We followed the Post downstream for about a mile, then turned west into the valley, which included a river flowing into the Post. As soon as we entered the valley we found bear signs everywhere, and very few signs of other game.

The game trail we followed evidently was an ancient bear trail, worn down by constant use. We saw many "barking trees", where bears had left claw marks for all to see. Bushes near the trail showed many wisps of brown grizzly hair. We proceeded very cautiously, feeling that the valley was certain to have inhabitants. By late morning we had not yet seen any wildlife, but a bit later Earl saw some movement on a high rocky shelf, which proved to be a black bear. We were following the left bank of the stream, while the bear was quite high on the right wall, on a small patch of meadow.

How to get to the bear was the question. We agreed that Earl would stay in his present position, where he could spot the bear, while I descended to the river, crossed, and climbed the opposite wall. This would take at least an half hour, so I got under way. I crossed the river, and arrived on the other side not too wet. With handholds, the climb to the meadow took about 25 minutes, and when I reached it, I turned to look for signals from Earl. Sad to relate, I could not see him from my position. So, with bear in mind I slowly moved thru the wooded meadow slope.

I located the bear, a large blackie, quite some distance from where he was first seen. The range was about 200 yards, and I decided a closer approach might spook him. So I squeezed off a shot. The bear started to run about in a very erratic manner, and then he sat down and, in a few moments, fell over. Shortly thereafter Earl appeared, and we went to the bear. Just to be sure we poked his eyes, and confirmed that the boar was dead. His pelt was glossy blue/black, in perfect condition.

We sat down for lunch and noticed three young rams on the top of the canyon, looking us over. They continued to do so until we moved out some time later. It was 3:00 p.m. before the bear was skinned and packed, and we were ready to move on. Before leaving, we glassed the slope carefully, and almost at once Earl yelled, "bear". It was another blackie, across the valley very near the point we had been when we sighted this bear. I didn't need another black bear, so we decided to start for camp, hoping to sight a grizzly en route. We saw none, but a beautiful caribou showed up, complete with a huge rack, and lovely white mane. He would have made a magnificent trophy, but I already had a caribou. So we went on our way, with sheep steaks in mind. We recrossed the Post without difficulty.

The news of bears across the Post, possibly somewhat elaborated, determined Jim's hunt the next day. He and Larry left early, with the left-over blackie in mind. They found the bruin very near the spot where I shot my bear. But since it got their wind, it was leaving rapidly, away from the river and up the steep side valley. The side valley actually was a canyon in profile, so Jim and Larry elected to go up the bottom, which consisted of a creek with many rock slides on both sides, and an occasional patch of meadow and alders. The boys, according to their account, sprinted up the creek bed to get ahead of the bear for a stalk. They had lost sight of the bear while running, and when they figured they were above the animal, they clambered up the side wall to make an interception. Unfortunately, the bear was uncooperative, and did not show. So after much searching, they gave up, and had lunch.

On their return down the creek bed however, the two suddenly found their bear, fast asleep, 50 yards ahead! Larry got the movie camera ready while Jim prepared to shoot. At this point the bear stirred, came awake, and stared at them. Since they didn't move a muscle, it looked at them for many minutes, then slowly began to leave. Jim signaled Larry, who started the camera, and Jim squeezed off the shot. The bear ran about 30 feet, received a second shot, and dropped. The sow was old and large, probably the one we had seen the previous day. Her pelt was beautiful. So ended this fine Alaskan foray.

CHAPTER II

THE CHUGACH, AND KODIAK

Goat Lake, the lake we were trying to find, was, not surprisingly, very difficult to spot. It was located at an altitude of 4100 feet in the high Chugach range east of Anchorage, and was less than a mile long. After some time in the air over the spot where the lake should have been, we went back to our check point, Klutina Lake, and tried again. This time the pilot of the twin Beech kept a close check on the compass heading, and we found the lake. From the air, and as we found later, from the ground, the area was a spectacular sight. It is the drainage basin for several small glaciers, and the mountains around the lake rise very steeply from its shores. For some time we saw no possible place where one could locate a camp, but near the outlet there was a very small patch of grassy ground. Sure enough, a couple of tents could be seen there, for our two packers

65

had been flown in the previous day to set up camp. On our way in, and as we now exited the area, we were greatly impressed by the Chugach. The peaks rise to about 16,000 feet, and in much of the area the access seems impossible. Snowy tops and glaciers are on all sides, and anyone who hunts there is in the toughest hunting country in North America. We wanted goat so Hal Waugh, our outfitter, said that here's where we'd find them. Actually, from the air we saw many goats. We were interested in bear too, but Hal said there would be very few here. However, we took care of that later. On our way out of the area we were in no hurry, and we found quite a few sheep, which was a matter of some interest, since three days of the sheep season were still available. In particular, found a band of nine rams, not far from out camp, on a neighboring mountain top. About an hour later, we arrived back at Anchorage International.

I had flown in by commercial air on September 6th, and Jack Simplot, my hunting companion, the "Potato King" from Boise, had met me at the airport. He had come up in stages from Boise in his twin Beech, with his pilot. At the hotel we met Earl Stevens, who guided me last year and would again this year. The packers, now at camp, were Larry and Marian Keeler, who were also with us last year. At this point everything was looking up, and we were quite excited about hunting in the area we had seen from the air.

We left the hotel the next morning with no idea we would get into camp that day. It was raining hard, and the ceiling was very low. We went to Lake Hood, and met our pilot, who was quite optimistic about making it today. He thought this was good flying weather, and, for Alaska, it was. Quite a number of light planes are lost each year in Alaska, and the morning paper, which we had picked up at the hotel, described three searches then in progress for down planes. The bush pilots we had flown with have been very meticulous, and I felt very comfortable flying with them.

The logistics of getting into our unnamed mountain lake, which we called "Goat Lake", were interesting. A Widgeon could not get in there, but a Cessna 180 on floats could, but with limited load because of the 4100 foot altitude, and short take off space. The lake was actually only three-quarters of a mile long, and had one landing strip — north/south. Because of some ice in the water, only about one-half mile was usable, and only from the north; the south end was blocked by mountains. So, you landed to the south, and took off to the north, regardless of wind direction. Fortunately the wind was usually from the north.

OUR LAKE IN THE CLOUDS

We left Anchorage about 9:30 from Lake Hood adjacent to Anchorage International. This is the only water strip in the country with a tower. The traffic is quite heavy, since the shores of the lake, perhaps two miles in diameter, are completely covered with parked seaplanes, wing-tip to wing-tip. Jack and Hal Waugh left about 15 minutes later in the Widgeon, with most of the gear. We both landed at Klutina Lake, altitude 2000 feet, which is only five minutes from Goat Lake, and provides a convenient staging point. There the passengers and gear from the widgeon were off loaded on the beach before being ferried 500 pounds at a time up to the little "Lake in the Clouds".

The weather was improving during the morning, and became quite acceptable late in the day. I went in first, without incident, and we taxied to a beach next to camp. The tiny strip of grass was adequate for the tents, but not much more. The Keelers had set up a six by 8 foot Whelen tent for food and duffel, and a beautiful eight by 10 foot wall tent, and an igloo style pop up tent which Hal and one of the packers used. All of these tents had self supporting frames, and they had to be held down with rocks at every corner. We were 2000 feet above the timber line, so we had no wood, or trees or stakes.

The cook tent was heated with a Coleman cook stove, and the tent which Jack and I occupied had a "Silent Sioux", a kerosene fired iron stove. Operating the Silent Sioux required great finesse, and caution. She had devious ways, which we discovered the first time we fired up. As soon as we lighted the stove, it started to pulsate in a very alarming manner. At the rate of about one per second, it would roar, and jump, nearly off it's base, with flames squirting out of every opening. It took some time to learn to control her strange manners, so that we could live with the lady. I wondered who had selected her name.

After we had gotten our tents and gear in some sort of order, if you can call it that in a tiny tent, we had a chance to look over our surroundings out-of-doors. The views were breathtaking in every direction. The mountains rose very steeply on the east side, where camp was located. To the south was a very beautiful group of snow capped mountains, with several small glaciers at their bases. The west wall also rose precipitously in a series of steps to at least 2000 feet above the lake. To the north was the opening in our horseshoe shaped valley, and it presented a panorama of great peaks. Our camp was located at the east edge of that opening. "Edge" is the correct word, because if you proceeded from camp about 40 feet, the terrain dropped very precipitously about 2000 feet to a broad valley below. We climbed that slope a number of times, and it was covered with a snarl of alders and stunted shrubs. The water in our lake was milky white in color. We didn't have to look very long for goats. There were quite a number of them looking at us from the top of the near vertical cliff to the east, about 2000 feet above the lake. I never tire of admiring the physical capability of an animal that can live where they live. Their instinct tells them that the only safe place for them is on a vertical cliff, so that is their preferred habitat.

The mountain goat bears little resemblance to the domestic goat — he is much larger, and belongs to the antelope family. The animal weighs between 200 and 400 pounds, and is very handsome. His coat is creamy white, and is very shaggy. His pelt is deep, with extremely fine hair next to the skin, and guard hairs on the outside. The animal appears to be wearing pantaloons, with thick leg hair all the way down to his hocks, where it terminates abruptly. His face is long and narrow, with large eyes, a long white beard, and short rapier-like horns which are quite breakable. Both the billy and nanny are almost identical in appearance. To see the animal negotiate what appears to be a vertical cliff is fascinating indeed. It is very deliberate, even when alarmed. Its eyesight is excellent, and, as we found out, so is its sense of smell.

After we had looked over our surroundings, we had a sandwich or two, and began to think of goats as game. There were some in sight above us at all times, and I didn't see any reason why we shouldn't go up there and polish a few off, since that's what we had come for. That turned out to be a very mistaken impression! But, Jack and Larry Keeler started up the mountain for a pair of goats on the left side, and Earl and I went for another pair, to the right. I thought the hunt might take as much as three and a half hours, and that we'd be back in camp for an early supper.

I was about to learn a lot about goat hunting. Actually, I had hunted goat before, but never in terrain as rough as this. The goat has survived by going places no one else can go. Where it lives it has no natural enemies. Any goat hunter must have in mind the vivid fact that risks are involved. After we had made a number of climbs, before taking the first goat, I used to have nightmares, thinking of some of the places I had been. Inching along a rock face is always iffy, but the Chugach rock is somewhat "rotten", and is prone to come off in your grip. But if you want a goat, there is no easy way. There are a few dividends, however. Between cliffs and crags are rockslides, which are a lovely feature of Alaskan mountains, and if everything is right, it's a great way to make a descent. Each step gives you, not 15 inches or so, but three or four feet, and, on the best shale sides, from 20 to 30 feet. If it continues to slide while you are standing still, you have to "hot foot" to a firmer area.

A series of rock slides down a mountain can be a delightful experience. However, there is one very serious problem. I recall seeing only one slide that extended from the top to the bottom of a mountain. Instead, a series of slides goes from top to bottom, and opportunely, you transfer from one to the other. An individual slide will terminate, against a rock shoulder, or, in a drop off. If it's a shoulder, you're lucky — you can see it. If it's a drop off, it is almost impossible to see it from above. The drop off may be several hundreds of feet, or more. I had some bad moments with this problem, until I learned that you had better get off the slide frequently, and take a look as to what is ahead — before you get there.

Another problem with goat hunting is the weather. Rubber or composition soled shoes, which are preferred, provide a firm grip on the rock, when it's dry. But when it's wet, you may have problems. The year we were in the Chugach, two goat hunters lost their lives on the Kenai Peninsula, which is flat compared to the Chugach.

GOATS, BUT —

It took about two and a half hours of hard climbing to get up near the shoulder, about 2500 feet over the lake, where the goats had been. Of course, they were not there. In that kind of terrain, there are a million places to hide, so we had to look — and look. We finally spotted them, at a range of about 400 yards. I was carrying a 300 Weatherby. I had the trajectory really nailed down out to 500 yards, so I was sure I could shoot a goat at 400 yards. However, the problem was not to shoot a goat. The problem was to shoot a goat that was not going to fall a thousand feet, and break up.

We followed a summit ridge for awhile, and thought

we had it made. Then, the summit ridge terminated in a vertical drop off. After a lot of looking we couldn't find any way to continue, so we went back and took a rockslide down the slope, on the side opposite the goats, and then again went over to the drop off. At that point we could cross the face, and did so, and came to a point where we should have been at the goat's level. At this point in the hunt, it became very clear to me that Earl could go anywhere the goat could go. And with Earl's guidance, I was going places that I would never have dreamed of going before. The Chugach is a great place to learn about rock climbing.

We soon found the goats, bedded down about 150 yards distant, and below our level. We looked them over for about 15 minutes with the binocs — we couldn't carry a spotting scope up there. Earl said that the one on the left was the nanny, and the one on the right was the billy. The billy's horns are heavier at the base, and noticeably so. As trophies there was no choice between them. Earl judged them to be, "better than 8 inches" — both excellent. Actually, quibbling about goat horns never made any sense. The difference between an average goat and a record book goat is a couple of inches. With sheep, it's a far different story.

So our task now was to avoid a hamburger goat — at the bottom of the cliff. The nanny was draped over a pinnacle just about the size of her body — forget her. The billy was on a small grassy patch — say eight by ten feet, pitched fairly steeply toward the drop off. Same problem. He was facing away from us, and Earl said the only way to get him was to break his back, to immobilize his hind legs, and thus avoid the push over the cliff. I was sure I could put the bullet in a two inch circle at that range with a prone rest, but where is a billy's backbone? The goat has a hump, like a grizzly, and a coat of about three or four inches of wool.

We finally decided to shoot back of and to the left of the hump. I squeezed off a shot, and a red spot appeared at the point of aim, but the billy lay still. The nanny leaped out of her bed and left. We thought we had the billy nailed, but after a few moments, he made a convulsive movement, started to roll, and went over the cliff!

The time now was 5:00 p.m. and we had to locate the billy to see if there was anything to take to camp. An hour later we had not found him, and, with darkness in mind, we decided to go to camp and find him the next morning. Earl and I were separated some hundreds of feet, and a gully lay between. I had a series of rock slides, that I descended very easily, and then I came to a point where I had about 100 feet of drop off. My legs were not as good as they had been that morning, and I was not too happy about my position. A neighboring slide looked good, but I wondered if it would still look good if I went there. I finally started to inch down the rock face below me, and found it was not quite so bad as it seemed from above. I was able to find firm hand holds all the way down. This took about 20 minutes, and the route below looked quite good, but my legs were nearly shot.

I finally got into camp about dark, and Earl arrived about 15 minutes later. He had found the goat in a gully he was descending, over half way down the mountain. It must have bounced and fallen over 1000 feet, and looked like it. He had skinned out the head and cape, and said the rest was mince meat. But, so was the cape. One horn was broken off, and the face and shoulders were perforated in dozens of places. The taxidermy job was impossible. Hal said he would put this goat on his license, if I wanted to try for another one. He did, and I did. But I was beginning to understand what I thought I knew. Goat hunting is tough.

The only thing I could think of, to do on the next opportunity, was to empty a magazine into the goat. They are by reputation very tough animals. Evidence in favor of that view is building up. Any animal that can survive an Alaskan winter on a mountaintop has to be made of cast iron - it is almost incredible. A short time later, Jack and Larry returned. They had an almost identical experience. The billy fell 1500 feet. They would look for him tomorrow.

Larry left early, and made a long hike around the base of the mountain to the north, and finally found Jack's goat. He brought back one horn, one hoof, and part of one hind quarter as the only salvage.

SCORE: ZERO

Thoughtful consideration showed that obtaining a fine goat trophy presented some unusually dificult obstacles. We licked our wounds, and discussed our options at some length. It is certainly possible to find a goat off his perch on the face of a cliff. This would however require much hunting on the mountain top, and the result would be pure speculation. Goats prefer the face of a cliff.

Jack decided he'd had his goat, and in the three days remaining of the sheep season, he'd go for a ram. The ones we had seen from the Beechcraft looked very attractive, and the mountain was "next door". So, he left next morning with the Keeler boys to establish a spike camp at the base of the mountain, next door. We learned, a few days later, that the sheep hunt had gone very well, and Jack got a fine ram.

I decided to continue working on goats, with no great conviction that the end of that road would hold a trophy. But, we'd try. Earl had much more optimism than I. He thought we could find one off its perch if we looked long enough. In the end he was right.

We left the next morning for the same area we had hunted the previous day. But we found a somewhat easier route to the top, by going down the shore toward the glaciers before starting our climb. At this point a series of slides extended all the way to the summit of the ridge which formed an almost straight backbone for the east mountain formation. We planned to work our way along this ridge for it's full length of about two miles, and scan the millions of rock gardens and patches of meadow below. The ridge was actually a knife edge, and at some points we found ourselves straddling the rock as we walked. By late afternoon, we had covered more than a mile on the ridge, and had seen no goats. So we returned to camp.

The next morning we elected to give the goats a day of respite, and to take a look at the main East/West valley below our lake for game, having in mind principally bears. Before we left camp that morning I suggested to Earl that he set up a goat stew for supper, since we had most of one hind quarter. He said that was not a very good idea, but there was no harm in trying the goat meat. So, he cut up some of the meat,

75

added the other ingredients, put plenty of water in the pot, and put it on the "back burner" of the cook stove. We descended the very steep pitch down to the valley below, and did see a single goat on the far side of the valley. In the manner of goats, he was perched on a cliff which, from this distance appeared to be quite vertical. I am sure that from the foot of the cliff it would not be that vertical, but it was very steep, in any event.

We spotted a number of other goats, but none within acquisition range. We saw no bears, but there were a few bear signs in the valley, both black and grizzly. The two can be distinguished quite easily in their footprints. The black bear's retractable claws do not "print", while the grizzly's non-retracktable claws print prominently. Just about dusk, in camp, Hal saw two goats on the cliff above camp, where we had found none the day before. That determined our destination for the following morning.

The goat stew gave off pleasant aromas, and I looked forward to a menu item that, to me at least, was new. When Earl said the stew was ready, it was easy to see that he had some reservations, and I soon found out what they were. The stew had a lovely flavor, and the vegetables were excellent, but when I tried to eat a piece of the goat meat, it resembled nothing so much as vulcanized rubber. I simply could not get my teeth into it, and I have my own teeth. It was incredible. I have since heard hunters say that they have eaten goat meat. Maybe the meat of a young kid can be eaten, but this meat from a mature animal was simply inedible. This fact gave me further pause, when I considered that the sheep and goats both live in similar areas of the mountain top, and one has the finest meat in the world, while the other can't be eaten. I was further distressed when I considered that in the laboratory we were spending very large sums each year in the search for new polymers with toughness, and other desirable qualities. If we could analyse the fiber structure of goat meat it might yield the key to polymer toughness!

We climbed that wicked peak again the next morning, by the glacier route. However, we had a problem almost at once. During the night, there had been a light snow on the tops, and rain on the lower slopes, which had frozen. While we were discussing the matter on the first day of the hunt, Earl said that we would not climb this mountain except in dry weather. But, we were desperate for a goat, so here we were, doing it. We rationalized the decision by saying that we would proceed very slowly, and expect that the sun would dry things out before we had to descend. After about two hours of climbing we got to a point where we could see the two goats of last evening. They were at a range of 300 yards and well above us, so we went back to work to gain altitude. Within an hour the range was down to 225 yards and we were able to look things over. The pair, a nanny and a billy, were trophy class. However, we again had a cliff problem. Where they were located the two were certain to fall if shot. While we were watching them, and chewing our fingernails, the pair slowly got up, and decided to take a mid-morning snack of moss and lichens. After awhile, they were out of sight, and Earl said we should undertake a stalk, on the chance that they were headed away from the cliff, to a grassy meadow.

Earl suggested that I remain there while he took a look. I dug my heels into the rock slide, about 200 yards below the summit ridge, and kept my thumb on the safety. An hour later, I heard a great clatter of rocks above me, and looked up to see two goats moving deliberately at the very crest of the ridge. If shot at that point, they would have to roll an untold distance down the slides. I left the safety ON. The goats were soon out of sight, and then Earl showed up, and said that he had inadvertently spooked the goats. In any event, things were looking up. At least two goats were off their perch.

We climbed to the summit ridge, found a place where we could sit down without hanging on with both hands, and had a sandwich. The goats were not in sight, so we wondered what came next. Earl came next, for he had spotted our two goats, apparently en route to the next mountain to the east. We considered trying to intercept the two, but we had no cover, and the possibility looked doubtful. They went out of sight under a shoulder of the mountain, and we decided that our mountain had just lost two goats. We took a noon siesta, and then considered our situation. We decided to go down the same far(east) slope of our mountain that the goats had taken.

WE EXPLORE A PASTURE

The valley there was a high basin; we could descend most of the way on slides, and we did. Almost immediately, I spotted the two goats. They were just crossing the stream in the bottom of the basin, on their way to the next mountain. We were about to take off for the goats when Earl spotted two other goats, on a shelf only a mile away. They were bedded down on a narrow lower ledge of a cliff, which offered no forage of any kind. From this ledge, we guessed, they could climb to a tiny meadow above to feed, or go down to the valley floor, with plenty of pasture. We had good cover for an approach, and we decide to be tricky. Earl would work his way over and above the goats, while I was getting into position below their shelf, in the lower meadow. When we were in place, Earl would descend on the shelf from above. There was no place for them to go but down, and I would be there.

We went together toward the goats, and after about a half mile, as we were about to take our separate ways we noticed the goats rise from their beds. If they went to the upper meadow, they were lost. But they looked things over for some time, and than started down. The goats were coming in our direction, and our task was to cover a half mile quickly, under cover, to a shoulder overlooking their route. Earl got there first, and I was right on his heels, out of breath, just in time to see the nanny walk majestically into sight, about 100 yards away. Then she got our scent, and stopped to consider things. While doing so, I touched off the .300 Weatherby, and put a 150 grain silvertip into her left shoulder. She toppled over, but like the tough goat that she was, got up, and required a second shot to keep her down.

Earl and I skinned the cape and pelt, and severed the hind quarters. We were ready to leave the area by 4:40 p.m. The pelt and horns were in perfect condition. But now, Earl and I had a new obstacle. We'd had a long and exhausting day, and we were a very long way from camp. We had the choice of going back up the steep slope we had descended for the goat, to the summit ridge, and from there down the precipice to camp. Frankly, we didn't have the strength to do it. Our only other alternative was to go north and around the shoulder of the mountain, to enter our camp from the north opening. It was a shorter route, but we had no idea if it was possible, for the north slope of our mountain was very steep indeed. So with no real alternative, we set out for the north route around the mountain.

Unfortunately, it was an extremely difficult route. The best part consisted of a very steep side slope covered with a tangle of alders. The worst parts were the precipitous ravines which cut the slope vertically at many points. And at one of these we nearly had a disaster. Earl was leading, and at one point he lost his footing, and started down a "no return" sheer slope. I was directly back of him, and I had a firm grip on a patch of alder with my left hand. With my right hand, I was able to grab the knapsack arm strap, and hold him, until he was able to establish footing and a hold. From that point, we inched across the slope, from one alder to the next one, with no free steps between. We got back to camp very late, completely exhausted. Even Earl's iron legs were out of business the next day. But, we had a goat!

THE SHEEP HUNTERS RETURN

Jack and Larry Keeler returned from their sheep spike camp. Their ram was not large but made a handsome trophy. Jack reported that the mountain where they hunted was "full of rams", and with more time one could find an exceptional trophy. Sheep hunting was not in our original plans, and the area clearly

"Lake in the Clouds". Chapter 2.

Cessna 180 on floats at "Lake in the Clouds" campsite. Chapter 2.

"Lake in the Clouds" campsite looking South. Chapter 2.

Scanning the peaks overlooking our Lake in the Clouds. Chapter 2.

On Kodiak after brown bear. Chapter 2.

Chauncey Guy Suits and Kodiak brown bear. Chapter 2.

Stone Sheep Country, B.C. Chapter 3.

Jack Simplot and packer at base camp. Note saddle boxes, not bags. Chapter 3.

Jack Simplot and ram. Chapter 3.

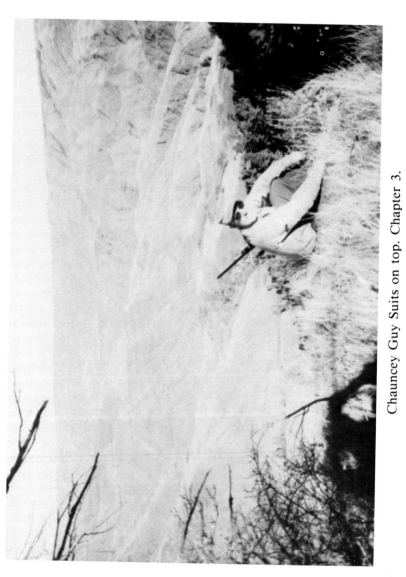

Chauncey Guy Suits on top. Chapter 3.

Jack Simplot, on top. Chapter 3.

Lynn Ross, on the constant search. Chapter 3.

Mount Kenny, 8368 feet. Chapter 3.

Our cook, at base camp. Chapter 3.

Base camp corral. Chapter 3.

Chauncey Guy Suits and Stone Sheep. Chapter 3.

deserved more attention. The Chugach range had produced all of the record rams, including the 1st place record holder at this time, which was taken just east of where we are hunting. Bush pilots had reported seeing astounding specimens when flying over the area. The trick is to get to them, and like the goats, they live where hardly anyone can go. Horses can't live in this country, so it's up to the man-on-foot. What he can carry on his back, and pack out, put the limit on his range, and for some of these blockbusters, that is not enough. Jack and Larry reported seeing numerous black bears, but all were sows with cubs.

We were still recuperating in camp while the Keelers went back to the spike camp to get the rest of the gear. During this period I had time to contemplate some of the aspects of back packing, and had been discussing it with my associates. One of the tents Jack Simplot used was the result of these discussions. Before describing it, however, let me establish some weight dimensions. A conventional tent which will comfortably accommodate two sleeping bags weighing from six to ten pounds. I had David Abercrombie, who is the best tent maker in our part of the country, build me "the smallest and lightest tent for two sleeping bags". It weighs three and three-quarter pounds. To try something new, I obtained some .002 inch mylar, which is sheet, transparent dacron, and Jim and I built two tents from this material. One of these tents, which comfortably holds three sleeping bags, weighs 15 ounces. Jack and party used one of these in their spike camp and reported that it worked very well. Strength of material was adequate. There was one odd quirk: the tents tend to "rattle" in a high wind.

WE'LL GO FOR BROWN BEARS

Next we held a council of war and decided to break camp. Fortunately, we had arranged to have a bush pilot fly in that day just in case we needed something. We did, we wanted to get out. Our reasoning was quite simple. I had a goat, and Jack was not trying for another. Jack had a ram, and the season was closed. We had seen no grizzlies. We talked the matter over with Hal, and decided to go to his camp at Deadman's Bay, on Kodiak, and try for brown bear. Hal seldom hunted there in the fall, because trophy bears seemed much easier to get to in the spring. But the camp was stocked and ready to go, if we could get there.

At 10:30 the 180 float plane came in. Upon hearing that we were breaking camp, the pilot radioed to his hanger, and asked them to send the widgeon for the moving operation. Jack and Hal then were flown down to Klutina Lake and off loaded on the beach, before the 180 returned for the two Keelers. Next, I and my gear was ferried. We went back to Klutina and picked up Hal and Jack, less all baggage, and left for Anchorage. Moments after we got there, the widgeon left for Klutina to pick up the rest of the party and all of the gear.

Now the trick was to get to Kodiak. North Pacific Airlines had scheduled flights to the town of Kodiak, and we could easily bush pilot from there, but they had no space for several days. A talk with a friendly bush pilot revealed that he could spare one of his three widgeons, to take us down, remain for one week, and then return. The price was high, but we swallowed hard, and engaged the trip. We would leave at 9:00 in the morning, which would give us three days of hunting, and one day to return.

AT DEADMAN'S BAY

We left Anchorage International nearly on time in beautiful weather, and landed in Deadman's Bay at 1:00 p.m. We had a great view of the Alaska Range on the way down, passed Afognak, and thence to Kodiak. As we approached Kodiak, it became clear that this was the bear's domain. From the air the island is laced with prominent bear trails, worn deep into the marshes from centuries of use. While we circled the camp area for a landing, we saw one brown bear nearby.

Hal's camp, a small cottage, was located at the inshore end of the bay, where a river enters. The bay is 15 miles long, and comprises a tidal estuary. One therefore has to note the tide, which is normally 18 feet, but according to Hal's table the tide today would be 21 feet. By the time we had chores done, and the camp shipshape, it was late afternoon, and we only had time to glass the area near camp.

The river which empties into the bay is the principal reason for a large local bear population. The spring and fall salmon runs, one of which was then in progress, choke the river with salmon, and make life easy for the bear. Relatively mild winters mean that the bear's hibernation period is much shorter than in the mountains. So the bears eat more, and for a longer period, and it shows in their size. We saw one bear about a mile distant, before it got too dark. We also saw many hair seals in the water, and made a mental note to take some, time permitting.

We wasted no time getting under way the next morning. Hal took Jack up the river, while Earl and I went for the river flats, which were very extensive. The day turned out to be foggy and overcast, so our visibility was quite restricted. At 6:30 a.m. we saw our first bear, a small yearling. The many streams which meander thru the flats were literally choked with salmon. The spawning salmon were making their way up the streams to die, and dead and dying fish were everywhere.

We crossed the marsh very slowly, and at Earl's advice, with the rifle at ready. Our paths were deeply rutted bear trails which criscrossed the entire area. About a half hour after entering the marsh, Earl spotted a large bear. It was quartering away from us, at somewhat more than 300 yards. Visibility was so poor, that we did not get a really good look at the animal before it disappeared into a patch of alders. We came up to the alders, and at about 100 yards from the patch, the bear came out. It spotted us immediately, but did not spook. Although concerned, the salmon had this bear's attention. It stood up to its full height of perhaps 8 feet, and looked us over critically. The bear tried to get our wind, but couldn't because of wind direction. After a few minutes, the bear again rose to full height, and repeated the same antics. While this was going on, I was in a quandary. The bear had beautiful markings, and would make a fine trophy, but Earl said that it was a small Kodiak bear. Because this was early in the morning of our first day, and we would undoubtedly see many more bears, I passed it up. We tramped the marshes all day, but saw only one more bear, and it was also a "small" one. Thereafter, we returned to camp, where we found Jack and Hal. The two were agog by their experience. They had seen a great many bears on the river, and Jack was absolutely fascinated by their antics in fishing, fighting and swimming, so he took reels of motion pictures of them, but didn't shoot any. There would be time enough for that in the next two days. The two planned to shoot one the next day, and so did we. It must be the "right" bear, of course, since we apparently had some choices.

WE "SELECT" A BEAR

We got out a bit late the next morning, and both parties went up the river to "select" a suitable bear. To tell the truth, we worked hard all day until dark, and no one saw a single bear all day! We now felt some concern for our reluctance to shoot a bear the day before. We only had one more day of hunting, and began to have some doubts about the outcome. Jack said that he had some great movies, and as far as he was concerned, he was not concerned. The next day he would hunt seal and king crab, and to heck with the bear. I decided I was still hunting bear, if we could find one. Just one!

After some discussion we left that last morning for Alpine Cove, several miles distant, which had one small salmon stream, and which had occasionally yielded bear. Hal had a small boat and an outboard which we used, and by 6:30 we were in sight of the Cove. While we were still a mile away I spotted a bear on the beach, with my binocs. We landed the boat, and took off thru the marsh to get close enough to evaluate the animal. At about 500 yards we looked it over carefully. The critter was a fairly large bear, and had a dark chocolate brown coat with tawny tips to the fur. Earl said it would "square" about 8 feet,

101

which would put the bruin in the moderately large class, for Kodiak. I decided that all points being considered, including the fact that this was our last hunting day on Kodiak, this bear would do.

Our range was very long, so we gained some more yards in the animal's direction. I wanted to shoot prone, and found a good spot before touching off three shots in quick succession with the .300 Weatherby. The boar went down with the first shot, I think my second shot went over his back, but I heard a loud "whomp" when my third shot reached home. I counted long paces as we approached the bear, and it added up to about 325 yards. The pelt was beautiful. I shot the bear at 6:35 a.m. and by 9:30 he was skinned out, and we were back at camp. There we measured the pelt, and Earl's estimate was right on the button; it squared eight feet exactly. Thus ended our bear hunt.

WE HAVE TAKE-OFF PROBLEMS

We had all of our gear on the beach for loading in the Widgeon by 7:00 a.m. The day was clear, but quite windy. Up to this point we had not become very well acquainted with our pilot. He was somewhat taciturn, and we were busy hunting. The flight down had been beautiful, without problems, and we were well satisfied with his performance. He supervised the stowing of gear, and we taxied out in preparation for take-off. By now the brisk wind had increased in intensity, and was kicking up quite a surf. The wind was blowing parallel to the Bay, and whitecaps topped the waves. It looked like too much sea to me. After some minutes of taxiing, the pilot said that we would have to wait for calmer water. So we taxied back to shore. He explained that the widgeon, with it's present load, could manage waves up to one foot, but the two to three foot waves we now had were a bit too much. The pilot scrutinized the situation very carefully with his one good eye. The other eye was artificial, we guessed. This should impair his depth perception, but we never observed any detrimental effect on his flying. I approved the deliberate and conservative attitude in the circumstances we were now facing.

The wind showed no sign of moderating, so what to do? The pilot knew the area very well, so he decided to take a look at Alpine Cove. He had in mind that a take-off from the head of the Cove, which was well protected from wind, would permit him to get off the water before meeting the high surf in Deadman's Bay. It was an attractive idea, which, however, required very careful planning. If the Cove were 500 yards longer, there would be no sweat, but it wasn't. The question was — could he get off the water before hitting the whitecaps. We taxied around the Cove for over a half hour, while the pilot studied the situation. He checked every section of the take-off run for obstructions, and he checked the wind intensity from different distances from the lee shore. Finally, the pilot was satisfied that a take-off was possible, so he turned us around at the extreme end of the Cove and shoved the throttles forward. Our bird slowly lifted off just before hitting the very rough water. A cheer could be heard in the passenger section. We had intended to stop at the town of Kodiak for gas, but high wind prevented this. So we stopped at Homer, which was Earl's home, in protected water. This pleased Earl very much, so he off loaded with his gear, and we continued on to

CHAPTER III
STONE SHEEP, AND SMOKE

I flew into Ft. St. Johns, B.C., via Toronto and Edmonton by commercial airlines, and joined Jack Simplot, who had come in from Boise, Idaho, with his own pilot and twin Beech. After a baggage hassle, we engaged a local pilot to fly us into Lynn Ross' ranch, some 150 miles to the northwest. We touched down at this beautiful spot in fading afternoon light. The pilot left immediately, and would return at 5:00 a.m. the next morning, to fly us into the base camp in the hunting area.

Jack won the toss, so he would go in on the Supercub's first trip. Accordingly, Jack was at the strip at 5:00 in the morning, but, sad to relate, the pilot and his Supercub were not there. Also sad to relate, the reason was quite evident. It had been a very dry summer, and forest fires were rampant in the region.

The air was very blue with smoke, and no pilot who expected to be among the survivors would fly into a canyon strip with that visibility. Jim showed up at about 11:00 a.m., with no mention of the 5:00 a.m. appointment, and now guessed that he might be able to get in — at least, he'd try. He did, with Jack aboard, and returned in about 45 minutes for me. We landed on a sand bar with no great problem. The Piper Super-cub was identical to one I was flying at the time, except that it had 24 inch balloon tires, (normally-12 inch) which were just great for a sandbar strip. So, here we were, in the Canadian Rockies, north of the Peace River, ready to start our first hunt for stone sheep.

In the view of many hunters, including myself, mountain sheep are the most desirable North American game trophies. And at the head of the sheep list, I would place Stone sheep. However, it is a close call. The Dall sheep are also magnificent, and for that matter, so are all of the big horn sheep. Stone sheep deserve a somewhat special mention, because of the Chadwick ram, which many hunters regard as the grandest North American trophy. This magnificent animal, with a point score of 196 6/8, is now in the national Collection. The #2 Stone ram, with a point score of 190, was taken in the same general area as Chadwick's, by Norman Blank, in the year following our present hunt, also guided by Lynn Ross.

At the time of this hunt, licensed B.C. guides were allocated a large section of mountain area, in which they had exclusive rights to guide out-of-country hunters. Native hunters could hunt there, but in the section which Lynn Ross controlled, the area was so rugged, and the access roads were so nearly impassable, that we never saw a native hunter.

In fact getting to the Lynn Ross ranch from New York State, was at least eventful. Airlines, at that time were very picky about baggage weight, and the excess baggage charge was excessive. To beat it, I shipped three duffel bags by rail, a month in advance. I got to Ft. St. Johns, via Edmonton, no problem. Then I began to look for bags and learned that there is no rail service to Ft. St. Johns. Shipments here came by rail to Edmonton, where they were given to truckers, who delivered them along the Alcan highway, to gasoline stations nearest the address location. I became very nervous. Without those bags, I had serious trouble. I found a large truck office in Ft. St. Johns, but the man had no record of my bags. After considerable discussion the office got on the phone, and much later located three bags at a gasoline station near Pink Mountain, which is a village of three houses, and, a gasoline station, 125 miles to the north. It's a long story, but the bags finally were picked up by Lynn's man, and brought to the ranch. As related above, Jack Simplot and I then engaged a bush pilot, recommended by Lynn, who flew us to the ranch.

Lynn's ranch is very impressive; it is located on the east foothills of the high Rockies in the area, about 25 miles west of Pink Mountain on the Alcan highway. It includes over a thousand acres, which embraces a very large clear valley with a 3000 foot grass landing strip. There is a very large and comfortable log cabin, and several guest cabins and a corral, all presided over by Mrs. Ross and her two daughters Marcia and Valerie. Lynn has over 100 horses, and he had taken a pack train of about 20 of them into the hunting area several days before our arrival.

The base camp area was very attractive. It was located by the bank of a brook, at the foot of an impressive cliff some 2000 feet high. Lynn and his crew had everything set up and ready. Jack and I shared a twelve foot by twelve foot tent with a sheetiron stove, and were very comfortable. Lynn's crew included his brother George, Jack's guide Pat Brady, and an excellent cook — Angus Harrold. Angus soon had some moose steaks on the fire, and immediately after lunch we took off to explore the area.

Jack and Pat went down the valley to the west, and Lynn and I went south for a few miles and then turned east into a very interesting valley which included Mt. Kenny, complete with a Matterhorn type profile, and a glacier on it's northwest facing slope. We scoped the tops repeatedly, but saw no sheep. The glacier had a number of caribou on it, all seeking relief from a rather warm August day. We left the valley by way of a game trail which led to a high basin leading north. We saw quite a number of caribou cows on the basin floor, and on a nearby side slope, a magnificent bull. He was lying down, and his antlers, still in the velvet, looked like a huge brush pile. With no sheep in sight, we entered a valley which led back to base camp, where Amos served some beautiful moose steaks for supper.

Jack got in a bit later, quite excited about some rams he had seen. Pat said that one of the rams was excellent, and Jack was tempted to take it. BUT, here we were, on the first day of a 21 day hunt, so Jack deferred, and I agreed with him.

Next day, we left camp at dawn, and were bothered by fairly heavy smoke. This reduced visibility a great deal, as well as contrast. Spotting a Stone sheep, against a rockslide in clear weather is a very speculative matter indeed, and with smoke in the air it's almost impossible. Lynn's eyes were the only antidote we had. Without his eagle vision I would not have seen many sheep. With them, we did quite well. Lynn decided that we would all go back into the area where Jack and Pat had seen sheep the previous day. He said that had been one of the most productive spots in his entire allotted hunting area, and it was so extensive that even two parties could not cover all of the basins and gullies in a single day. We rode about three hours to get into the area, and the last hour was very rugged indeed.

The game trail we followed climbed very steeply thru a rocky spruce-covered slope. Every few minutes, we would have to dismount, remove our rifles for fear of breaking them, and let the horses battle their way upward. Western ponies must have learned something from mountain goats, because they climbed the same way and with the same determination. The climb from the valley floor was about 3000 feet vertically, and led to a beautiful high basin with many meadows and mountain streams. The surrounding peaks extended up to 9000 feet. It was a great place for sheep.

As soon as we got to the tree line, which marked the start of the basin, we tied the horses. Then Lynn spotted a band of seven rams. They were bedded down about three-quarter mile away, well above us, placidly chewing their cuds. We set up spotting scopes and looked them over carefully. The smoke pall was quite a problem, but we were able to see well enough to make sure that there was no ram larger than three-quarter curl in the lot. With spotting scopes, we then located three more rams, one of which had a respectable full curl, which, however, was not of trophy quality. Late in the day we started back to camp on the same rugged trail we had ascended earlier, but in reverse. It wasn't any easier. The only consolation was those beautiful moose steaks, which were excellent and numerous. After dinner, Lynn discussed plans, and said that he would move the pack train tomorrow about 20 miles to the southwest, to an area which had not been hunted in recent years. It sounded like a great idea.

It was about 7:00 a.m. before the pack train was ready and under way. But Lynn preceeded us by about two hours to do some trail cutting. To get to the camp area, the pack train had to climb another very steep, very rugged slope. The route was a moose trail thru a nearly impenetrable tangle of spruce, rocks and alder. Without the cutting Lynn had done, it would have been impossible. All of the packs took very hard beatings, as the horses pulled their loads thru narrow stubble lined passages, just wide enough for a horse. In spite of a heavy tarp cover, one of my bags was torn open at the zipper, and a second was ripped at a main seam. I began to give full credence to Lynn's statement, "where no one has hunted in recent years". After some hours we finally gained the tree line, where we set up camp, built a corral, and had some more moose steaks for dinner. Pat spotted a single ram on the skyline just before dark.

In the morning, Jack and his guide, Pat, left by horse for the southwest, while Lynn, George and I left on foot to climb to the summit ridge just east and above camp. Lynn's brother George, does not regularly guide for Lynn. George is an oil well construction worker, whose principal employment is during the winter, on the tundra. This was his off season, and he came along partly for the fun, and partly to get some pictures for Lynn. He had a fine Rolex movie camera, and was interested in getting some hunting pictures that Lynn could use during his off season, when he usually went south to talk to prospective customers. This was an unexpected bonus for us, because we later got some copies of some of his best pictures. Also, the hand-held walkie-talkie had just come to market, and I brought four units with me to try them for hunting. That was a new idea at the time, and we had some rather original experiences with them.

As we climbed up the ridge it soon became clear that this was where the ewes lived. We came upon many bands of them, numbering from a few ewes, to one band of 29. But we saw not a single ram. It is well known that, except during the rut, sheep ewes and rams prefer to go their separate ways. They like it that way. When we returned to camp later, Jack had a similar experience, except that they had also seen two very small rams. So, we had to face a fact of nature, and conclude that the rams were somewhere else. So, after a conference, Lynn decided to move back to the high plateau, where we HAD seen rams, but not the right ones. A great many rams were in that area, and we'd have to take a more careful look. Instead of going back to our comfortable base camp, we'd set up camp just below treeline at the plateau, and save five hours riding. I have been on many pack train trips, but I still continue to wonder at the mobility of the system. Almost anywhere you want to go, you can go, and set up a comfortable place to eat and sleep, and contemplate the majesty of the mountain landscape.

RADIO FOR A RAM

Next morning, both parties left on foot, and climbed into the beautiful basin. We were surrounded by high peaks, and this basin was a huge amphitheater, mostly open to the east, and extending up to the high ridges at the other three points of the compass. The basin was covered with a tangle of low spruce and alders, and included many narrow dry washes extending upward toward the ridges. We immediately saw some rams, and the spotting scope showed at least seven in view at the moment. One of the rams, in a band of four feeding down one of the washes, had a very respectable full curl. After much discussion, Jack decided that this ram would fit his requirements, so we laid on a strategy.

The sheep were on a high shoulder to our right as we faced the basin, about one and a half miles from our position. They were feeding slowly down a dry wash where the tree line tangle of spruce and alders was about five or six feet high, so visibility was restricted. We decided that this was a great opportunity to make a walkie-talkie stalk. So, we synchronized our watches, and agreed to a contact by radio every quarter hour. Jack and Pat took off, and they were lost to sight almost immediately in the tangle of alders. From our vantage point, with the spotting scope, we could maintain a fairly good line on the rams. But keeping a line on the hunters began to look hopeless.

At the first quarter hour contact, Jack reported that they hadn't seen the sheep since they had entered the alders. We then discovered something that saved the day. We couldn't see the hunters, but when they extended their antenna, the sun reflection from their chrome plated shaft could be seen. We were then in this situation. We had a line on the hunters, and the sheep, and they could not see us or the sheep. After about three contacts, things began to become interesting. We guided the hunters to a point where we judged that they must be on the same dry wash the sheep were descending. Jack was fully alerted, but said the sheep were not in sight. A few minutes later, a shot rang out! Within a few minutes, Jack reported that he had taken the full curl ram at about 100 yards. It had a beautiful tight curl, and he was very pleased with the trophy.

We can't prove that this was the first ram taken with the benefit of portable radio, but it must have been among the first. After some years, the use of walkie-talkies for mountain hunting raised questions concerning sportsmanship, with which I agreed. But at the time, that question had not arisen

After the ram was dressed out and aboard the pack train, we returned to our base camp area, where we had left our supply cache. We set up camp and made plans for the next day, while munching moose steaks. We would have ram backstrap the next day.

BIG RAMS, EVERYWHERE!

We were away shortly after daybreak, headed back to the southeast basin, where, some days before, we had seen three rams. There had been booming thunderstorms all night, and we were delighted to find that the smoke had pretty well washed out, leaving the best visibility we had had thus far. About two hours later we were at the timberline entrance to the basin, and had five rams in the spotting scope. While looking them over, Lynn spotted twelve rams on the opposite side of the valley. They were about one and half miles away, but even at that distance, some massive heads were in evidence. So, we tied the horses and took off for the large band.

We had perfect cover in the spruce for about a mile, and then we climbed a series of creek beds and washes, until we ran out of cover. We were then about 700 yards from the rams, who were bedded down on a high rocky shoulder just above the upper limit of a grassy meadow. In the spotting scope, I saw several exceptional rams, and one in particular was the best I had ever seen. However, we were at the lower edge of the meadow, and had no place to hide. There was no other approach in sight. The meadow was moderately steep, but fairly uniform in slope, with only few widely scattered spruce and alders for cover. So, with no alternative, we put our rifles between our elbows, and crawled on our tummies, very slowly, with our heads low.

We finally got to within 500 yards of the rams, and decided that we had run out of space. The exact distance, at "about" 500 yards, is very important. The trajectory of my 7 mm Weatherby, with a 154 grain Hornaday, and 76 grain #7828 is:

Range (yds) 0	100	200	300	400	500
Drop (inches)	+3	+3	-3	-17	-40

Thus, my 7mm Weatherby is a 400 yard rifle. I had calculated the trajectory, and measured it on my own range with the handloads I was now using. The exact distance is another matter. I have used range finders for this purpose, but the accuracy of those gadgets is poor beyond 200 yards. A better method is to calibrate the riflescope image.

Calibrating a riflescope image works out this way: Adjust the power of your scope so that, at 100 yards a 6 foot ruler just fills one-half the diameter of the image. On the scope I am now using, that's 8X. SIX FEET, because that is ABOUT the length of the body of a ram, a goat or pronghorn, and so forth. With that calibration, if you have an animal in the scope, as seen sidewise, which just fills one-half of the field, he MUST BE AT 100 yards. If his image fills one-fourth of the field, he must be at 200 yards, and if it is one-eighth of the field, he is at 400 yards, and so forth. See the diagram below.

WITH SCOPE SET TO 8X

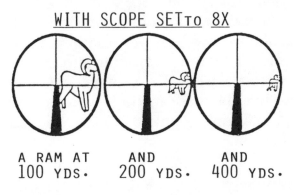

A RAM AT 100 YDS. — AND 200 YDS. — AND 400 YDS.

We studied the range of the rams at length. Lynn guessed 400 yards, but my measurement said 500 yards. While all of this arithmetic was in progress, I was fairly drooling over the largest ram in the band. He had at least one and a quarter curl, widely flared, with massive bases. It would have to go to 170 or 180 points.

We watched the rams for about a half-hour, thinking they might feed down the slope, but when they got up, and it looked like they might feed upward, I decided to shoot. I had a bipod rest, and a steady aim. I asked Lynn to call the position of the shot in the spotting scope. When the ram was sidewise, I placed the crosshairs 30 inches above the ram's shoulders, and two feet to the left, which seemed to be the windward, and squeezed off. Lynn reported that the range was perfect, and that the shot landed exactly shoulder high, but 6 feet to the right. When we got up to the shoulder where the ram had been a few minutes before, the reason was clear. There was a crosswind of about 20 knots over that shoulder. In the lee, where we had been, there was almost no wind. Pity! So, after all the perspiration, and arithmetic, the final answer was zero. I have never seen a better ram.

The rams ran up the slope and headed for a high ridge. Lynn said we might intercept them by climbing to a saddle just north of our position. We did, and saw them well out of range, going into an escarpment overlooking a glacier. We spent a couple of hours in the area, but didn't see anything worth shooting. We got back to camp, exhausted, and ate huge quantities of steaks from Jack's ram.

The following day the weather continued warm and clear, with only a slight smoke haze. Lynn wanted to go back to the same basin we had hunted the day before and I couldn't agree with him more. That was certainly where the rams were. So, in about two hours we were there, and had the same band of five rams in the spotting scope. The band of twelve was nowhere in sight. Our band of five included two full curls, one of which was very impressive. His right horn was one and a quarter curl, but the left horn had been broomed back about three or four inches. The bases were massive, and we judged that he might make the record book. The band was feeding about 800 yards above us, on a steep grassy meadow.

There was no cover for a direct approach. But 200 yards to our left was a dry wash going up the slope, with excellent cover, if we could get to the dry wash. To do so required a belly crawl thru low brush and grass. We alternated in the crawl. One man crawled as long as the sheep had their heads down, feeding. Then we froze when the animals raised their heads. Then the other man crawled, while the first man watched the sheep, and so forth. It took some time to gain the cover of the wash, but we did so without alerting the sheep. Then we started our climb, on tip-toes.

We had gone but a short way up, when we discovered three more rams above, directly on our intended path, and one of them had a beautiful set of one and a quarter curl horns, with no brooming. We had no cover to approach the three rams, so we lay motionless until, about an hour later, they bedded down. We crawled out of sight, and found a spruce slope, with the wind in our favor, that let us gain a shoulder, overlooking the three rams. When we peered over the shoulder, the rams were gone! We never did see these rams again. They just went someplace else, before we got up to their position. Disappearing is one thing rams are good at.

We believed we still had a chance to get to the original band of five rams. We were now well above the position in which they were last seen, but they were no longer there. We slowly walked thru some spruce above the meadow in which the rams were feeding, until we came to a steep escarpment which dropped away very precipitously. We peered over the edge, and about 200 yards directly below us were the five rams. The big one was in plain sight and he looked magnificent, but if he were shot in his present position he would have fallen at least 1000 feet. Then at that exciting moment, the sheep saw us, and they had a problem. They couldn't go to the left, because of the cliff. We blocked their upward flight, which is usually their preference. Their only flight path was back toward the meadow, directly under and in plain sight of our position. I had an excellent view, and kept the crosshairs on the big ram as he ran across the slope below, at a distance of about 200 yards. Lynn became very nervous, because I held my fire, but I was sure the ram would stop for a look, and he did, and he got a bullet in the right shoulder.

The ram rolled about 500 yards down the steep grassy slope before coming to a stop, without damage to horns or cape. The right horn measured 41 inches, and both bases went to 14 and a half inches. He finally ended up in the Boone & Crocket Records with a score of 166 7/8 points. When we got back to camp some time later, Angus very thoughtfully broiled some more of those delicious sheep steaks from Jack's supply, which were even better when served with hot buttered rum, which, somehow, was found in the packs. Half way thru the dinner, George, who had been out alone all day for photographs, rushed into camp, and said that there was an absolutely massive ram less than a half-hour from camp. He was bedded down, and an approach to within 100 yards was possible. Since we already had two rams, we could only congratulate George on his discovery. His photographs later confirmed that it was a possible record breaking animal. I presume this could have been the second place ram that Lynn's hunter got the next year in the same area.

After dinner, when no one was feeling any pain, George told us about an interesting local phenomena known as the Stampede. He emphasized that this was not to be confused with a Rodeo, which is regarded as sissy by the guides. It is organized informally each year when all of the guides, packers and outfitters are in Ft. St. Johns buying supplies for their fall hunts. In the recent one, George won (1) The wild horse race, (2) The wild mare milking contest, and (3) was second in the wild cow milking. As George explained, it became clear that these are NOT sissy affairs! In the wild horse race, the idea is to ride a completely unbroken horse in the shortest time between two judges. The horse wears a single rope at it's neck, and no halter, saddle or other gear is allowed. Two men work as a pair in this race. George's winning method is the following: At the starting gun, his partner grabs the rope and throws his arm over the horses head, and covers both eyes. He then bites one ear, which, George explained, stops the horse momentarily. George then climbs aboard and guides the animal by cuffs on either side of the head. Very few riders finish the course. George attended the Edmonton Rodeo last year, and fell asleep watching it. It's not in the same league with the Stampede.

We decided to move back to base camp in the morning, restore supplies, and then move to the Mt. McCusker elevation (8393 feet) area for goats. We knew this would be fairly routine, because George had said that, "goats are no problem". We had trophies in mind, but not record book heads, which in any case, aren't found in this area. Angus had remained at Base camp during our sheep detour, and explained that Jack and his guide Pat had left for goats a couple of days previously.

WE GO FOR GOATS

We took off for goats the next morning, but about an hour on the trail, we met Jack and Pat — they were returning from goat camp. They hadn't seen a single goat, and after two days looking, Jack lost interest. They were returning to base camp. We had arranged for our pilot to come into base camp at the end of ten days, to see if we needed anything, and Jack decided to fly out with him. As soon as that became clear, we rearranged our plans. Lynn would have to go back with Jack to check out his trophy with the game warden, and arrange an export license. Pat and George would go on with me, with goats still in mind. As we did so, I had my fingers crossed at this point on the idea that, "goats are no problem". Every goat that I had hunted had not only been a problem, it had been a nightmare. I just couldn't imagine a "no problem" goat. And it was especially strange that Pat and Jack had not seen a single goat.

We saw no goats on the way in to what became our goat camp. But it was a beautiful spot, with high peaks in all quadrants, and it was fun to be there even without goats. But, with goats in mind, we left at dawn the next day to explore neighboring basins. Pat took a basin to the southwest, and George and I went for a large basin to the east. When we compared notes around the campfire that night, we had real concern.

Pat had seen two goats. But the river bottoms, which were usually tracked up, had no fresh tracks at all. The area had been populated by large bands in previous years. The goats were somewhere else.

With few alternatives to consider, we decided to take a look at the two goats that Pat had found, on the theory that two goats were better than none. The proof of the theory is almost self evident. We left camp before dawn, in a light rain, and entered the basin where Pat had seen the goats. There are a number of difficulties in hunting goats, but the worst is well known. The goat is defenseless against the timber wolf, and over the generations has learned that survival depends upon living on vertical cliffs, where the wolf can't go. In the Alaskan Chugach, while sheep hunting, I observed three goats on a vertical cliff, where they remained for ten days. Eventually, they ran out of local food, and had to come down, but they hated the idea.

The basin we were entering was about five miles long, with a large snow field at the far end. The area to the left was steep and rocky, and the right side was mostly vertical cliffs, with some steep grassy meadows at the foot. Almost at once, I spotted a goat on the right wall, and a bit later George found one nearby. The animals were well down the valley, near the snow field, and we made our way down there and discussed our situation. From many sad experiences I had learned that a goat shot on a cliff is a goat lost. They invariably fall or jump, from the cliff, and end up below in a mess that even a skilled taxidermist cannot unscramble. Unlike sheep, goat horns are very breakable. As previously mentioned, on an Alaska hunt Jack shot one goat, and ended up with a horn and a hoof, which he had mounted as a trophy. He was lucky to find any unbroken horns. So, with all this in mind, we looked at our goats. I climbed within 100 yards of one of the goats. If shot, he would have fallen about 800 feet vertically, so I just looked. The goat's instinct not only repels wolves, it repels hunters. Lynn's remarks, "goats are no problem", came to mind. We watched for a long time, but in the end we went back to camp. Around the campfire, later, we agreed that the goat was not an endangered species. The goat is going to survive for a long time.

While we were enjoying the warm glow of the campfire, George remarked that, after all, we were lucky — we had gotten back to camp. George had great stories, and I was sure that was the prelude to one of them. George's father, R. Lynn Ross Sr., now retired, was a famous guide in this part of the Rockies for a long period of years. In 1936 he had an Austrian Count as a client, on a six-week hunt for sheep, and everything else available. According to George, his Dad and the Count were three days out of their base camp, with two horses and one pack mule, when it began snowing heavily. They made camp for the night, and by morning there were two feet of snow on the ground, and it was still snowing. They started back to base camp, but by the end of the second night, they were pretty well immobilized by 4 feet of snow. It continued snowing, and they realized that they were in a desperate situation. The horses were unable to make any headway in the deep snow, and they had only a small supply of food. What to do? Ross Sr. shot one of the horses, and cut the hide into thongs. With tree boughs and the thongs, he made two pairs of snowshoes. It took them 10 days to get back to base camp. After hearing the story, we stopped being sorry for ourselves.

Later that evening, we decided that our plan would be to return to the basin every morning until we caught the goats off the cliff. If we should be so lucky, we might shoot one, or two - two per license was allowed.

The next morning we entered the basin, tied the horses, and slowly made our way toward the snow fields at the far end. About a mile from the snow field, we found the goats. They were off the cliff, and bedded down on a ledge at the foot, at a range of about 700 yards, and we had no cover. So we decided to go into the spruce and move toward the snow field, in the hope that there might be an approach from that side. About 30 minutes later we came out of the spruce, to find that the goats had left their ledge, and moved down into a small patch of meadow at the foot of the snow field. They were clearly in a shootable position, providing we could get within range.

We had the goats about 500 yards from our present position, and I wanted to get down to 400 yards, if possible. We had absolutely no cover, only a grassy meadow between us. The "move-when-they-feed, and freeze-when-they-look method seemed to be the only option open, so we tried that. George got his camera set, with the 6 inch lens, and we both lay on our backs in the grass, with our feet toward the goats. I cradled my rifle on my tummy, and we moved slowly, one at a time. I moved when the goats were feeding, with heads down, while George watched. The moment he saw their heads come up, or one head come up, we froze, and so forth.

We gained somewhat more than 100 yards this way, when, suddenly, the goats took alarm, and started toward the snow bank. I took a comfortable prone position, and when the rear goat stopped to look back, I let off a shot. I heard the bullet "plop", and he rolled to a stop. The second goat was rapidly getting out of range, so I gave him one shot, which broke his right front leg, and a second shot that anchored him. The post mortem showed that the range was 450 yards I was delighted to find that George had gotten the entire sequence with the Rolex, and I was able to get a copy later.

Both animals had fallen on the snow, and horns and pelt were in perfect condition. The horns of both animals measured nine and one-eighth inches, but their ages were five and nine years. The five year goat had six front teeth, all very loose, and the nine year old had three, about to drop out. We wondered whether a mouth disease, which took a terrible toll of Dall sheep some years ago, was responsible for the shortage of goats.

The following day our pack train returned to base camp, where we left by Supercub, for Ft. St. Johns, and home. It had been a fabulous hunt.

CHAPTER IV

THE ALASKA GAME HIGHWAY

Bears and caribou can be hunted almost everywhere in Alaska. But not all parts of Alaska were created equal. Equal in size of the animals, their abundance in a given area, and their accessibility. We had hunted in many parts of Alaska and were exploring the Alaska Peninsula for the first time. The peninsula proper extends SW of Anchorage for about 500 miles, and the Aleutian Islands extend westward in a great arc for an additional 1000 miles. The Peninsula is a vast area, and a great game highway from one end to the other. In a given hunt, which we were now on, we could only explore a tiny segment of this fascinating place. We were bound for King Salmon, which is located on the west shore of Lake Besharoff, about 300 miles from Anchorage. King Salmon has an Air Force base, and it can be reached by local commercial air. The airport is a favored staging point for sportsmen headed south, and we expected to meet Park Munsey, our outfitter, there.

Park lived on Kodiak and hunted out of his home for bears, and had a number of additional camps at various points on the peninsula. We first met Park many years previously, when he was packing for Hal Waugh at Post Lake, in the Alaska Range. He later went into business for himself, and attained the Master Guide status. When that guide rating was first established, Hal Waugh obtained the #1 certificate, and it was richly deserved.

We got into King Salmon in late afternoon, in marginal weather, and expected to meet Park the next morning. He would be flying in from Kodiak in his Cessna 180 on floats. We were advised that we could stay at the "Inn", so we checked in. The marginal weather surprised no one here. The typical weather in Alaska is BAD, but the typical Peninsula weather is TERRIBLE. Our party was comprised of Jack Simplot (Chm. J.R. Simplot Co., Boise, Idaho), and Bill Aydelotte (Chm. Ayco Corp., Albany, N.Y.) from Schenectady, N.Y. I will not attempt to cite a VITA on these two eminent gentlemen — it would be very impressive indeed. We had hunted together for years.

The Inn could give us rooms for the night, and we engaged them. It was not a plush hostelry, so we simply put our sleeping bags on the not too fancy beds, and remembered that for the next two weeks we would not even have these beds, nor indoor toilets.

Actually, we had somewhat more urgent matters on our minds, and although we knew in advance that the weather here would be awful, we began to wonder whether the two weeks we had allocated would give us enough hunting time. It was too late to make a change now, so we could only hope for a few breaks in the rain and fog. We were lucky to have Park's plane with us during the hunt, for without it our mobility would have been very limited indeed. The peninsula has a ridge of hills and low mountains on it's extreme eastern edge, but the balance of the area is a continuous bog, with innumerable lakes and ponds. Bears are found mostly in the eastern foothills, while caribou and moose live in the bogs and muskegs.

Lake Besheroff is roughly an oval with a 56 mile E/W axis, and about 30 mile N/S. A small outlet creek empties into Bristol Bay to the west, and a long narrow bay extends south from its SE corner for about 20 miles, and we would be located down this bay. Park did get in the next morning, and said that he was docked on a slip on the creek, quite near the airport. Since we would be flying with him a good deal in the coming weeks, I was interested in checking out his equipment, so we went down to the creek. At the time, I was flying a Cessna 185, about 600# gross heavier than the 180, on amphibious floats, and was quite familiar with the 180. In addition to the Cessna, I was also flying a Grumman Widgeon flying boat, so I was well acquainted with water flying.

THE MORES OF THE FLOAT PLANE

Since we would be in the middle of float plane problems in the days ahead, I had better explain what these problems are. They are numerous, but the number one float plane problem is: the floats leak. If floats were used only in fresh water, the seams could be welded and they would not leak. In salt water, however, aluminum corrodes rapidly, and the only known protection is an anodized film. This film is applied electrically, like silver plating. If the sheets were welded together, it would destroy the film, so they are riveted together with a fabric separator. This joint preserves the anodized film, but leaks. Each float, like an ocean liner, is sectionalized, so that a bad leak in one compartment will not sink the ship. Each section, usually ten per float, has to be pumped out occasionally thru an access tube which extends to the bottom. If the floats are well maintained, a continuous water exposure for one day might yield a pump-out of a quart or so — no problem.

I have mentioned the Aleutian weather, in fairly harsh terms. But they weren't harsh enough. Park intended to leave the next morning for the 45 minute flight to our camp on the south bay of Besharoff, but the cloud bank was right on the deck, and delays were indicated. It was raining continuously, with a wind of 30 knots which did not help in the least. All we could do was to shuttle between the dock, where our gear was piled under plastic sheets, and the Inn, and hope for improved ceilings. Between shuttles, we were distressed to find that someone had stolen two cases of beer from our cache. This grave deficiency was remedied immediately by obtaining two more cases, which we stowed aboard the 180.

Shortly before noon, Park announced that we had flying weather. However, our ceiling was about 150 feet when we finally approached the camp area, Park landed without incident in a fairly high sea. He taxied to a shore which had a short strip of sand beach, where

Chauncey Guy Suits and two beautiful mountain goats. Chapter 3.

DeHaviland Beaver float Plane. Chauncey Guy Suits and Jim Suits. Chapter 5.

Multiple tributaries of the "Icy Post" River. Chapter 5.

Looking north from base camp. Chapter 5.

Base camp on a work day. Chapter 5.

Dave Suits with naval binoculars. Chapter 5.

A beautiful spike Camp in the spruce. Chapter 5.

Base camp caught in an August snowstorm. Chapter 5.

Left to right: Dave Suits, Earl Stevens, Chauncey Guy Suits, Jerry (last name unknown). Chapter 5.

Left to right: Jerry (last name unknown), Dave Suits, Joe Delia. Chapter 5.

Larry Keeler fleshing out a ram cape. Chapter 5.

Jim Suits and ram. Chapter 5.

Chauncey Guy Suits with face-to-face grizzley. Chapter 5.

Partial roster: top: Jerry (last name unknown), Chauncey Guy Suits, Jim Gartin; bottom: Dave Suits, Joe Delia, Earl Stevens; missing due to flood delay: Larry Keeler and Hal Waugh. Chapter 5.

Fully loaded pack train heading into Stone sheep country. Chapter 6.

Looking down from above in Stone sheep country. Chapter 6.

his man, Bill, was waiting. Tie downs consisted of two junk auto engines, and these lovely objects anchored the plane with the floats high on the beach.

Our camp was a double-walled cabin, complete with a cook stove and bunks. We found the cabin to be quite weatherproof and comfortable. Our firewood was driftwood, but there was an abundant supply, so getting dried out around the stove became a daily delight. Our Bill, Bill Aydelotte, we now had two Bill's, reported that he had seen several moose, and a number of caribou, and, across the bay, three bears. Park's Bill, was an Aleut, who met us on the beach. Our crew included Earl, an experienced guide who would work with Jack, and Ed, a personable young ex-marine who would do the cooking. Ed prepared an excellent dinner, served with beer, after which there was very little intellectual discussion. We fell into our sleeping bags for the night.

RAIN, AND RAIN

Next morning we awoke to the sound of driving rain, and it was clear that hunting on the peninsula was going to be tough. After breakfast, we decided to give it a try. That meant full rain gear, which included waders that came to the chest, a hooded parka, tightly tied around the neck, and rubber gloves. The wind was at least 40 knots, and the rain fell horizontally, not vertically. Visibility into the wind was zero, and in the lee, not much better. Binoculars were worthless, and we didn't even try a spotting scope. We only made a few hundred yards from the cabin when we concluded what was obvious — we couldn't hunt today. On the way back to the cabin we noted many mallards in the bay. Park said that, at that time of the year, they feed on dead salmon, and were not worth shooting.

The next morning we remembered that we came here to hunt, so we again decked out in full rain gear, from head to toes, and ventured out. We spotted a sow with two small cubs across the bay, and on our side not far from camp, a sow with two mature cubs. After about an hour, with the wind somewhat higher than the day before, and heavy continuous rain, we had to conclude that hunting conditions were again impossible. So, we returned to camp for the day. That gave us plenty of time for camp chores, but we didn't have any. A certain feeling of dissatisfaction concerning the weather could be noted among the hunters. It is ordinarily referred to as profanity.

Next morning we were desperate. We hadn't yet been hunting, and the weather, which was moderating slightly, was still miserable. We decided that, come what may, we were going to hunt. Earl and Jack left along our shore, heading easterly, and Park and I left on the windward shore, headed south. About a mile from camp, the rocky shore changed to a hard gravel beach with excellent footing. Continuing south on the beach, we sighted something about a mile ahead. With glasses fully covered by rain drops, and binocs useless, we could only speculate on what it was. Continuing south, the first guesses were — a caribou. The color was right, but the animal was wrong. It turned out to be a tawny colored bear, fast asleep on the beach. It was a small bear - Park guessed the hide would square 7 feet, but, his pelt was beautiful. His back was a very light silvery gray, and his legs and underbody were very black. He was the most handsome bear I had ever seen. We approached to about 100 yards, and discussed its future. I had in mind a larger bear, and with much regret, I decided to pass this one up. So Park and I started up a nearby creek in search of other game.

We hadn't gone far, however, when Park stopped, and said he would like to take another look. He did, and said that in all of his years of hunting, he had never seen a more beautiful bear.

So, Park took another look at the bear. After some minutes of consideration, he finally decided NO, and we resumed our hunt. The bear was still fast asleep. We hadn't gone very far, however, when I began to have second and third thoughts concerning the bear. I reasoned that I might never again see a bear with its striking coloration, and, who wants a great big bear in the standard dark brown? So, I shot the bear, and I still get a thrill out of that beautiful trophy.

When we got back to camp with the head and pelt, Jack and Earl also returned, and reported seeing only sows with cubs. The two Bills came back with some exciting news. They had found a rather big bear that they judged would square at least nine and a half foot. The bear was shot at the edge of a creek, and had rolled into the water. The two Bills couldn't move it enough to start skinning, so they opened the bear up, and would go back the next day with more manpower. They were delighted with the large animal.

Next morning Park took the bear crew to the site, and spent most of the day managing the pelt and head. We were greatly cheered to see some moderation in the weather. The wind had gone down a great deal, and the remaining showers were quite manageable. Jack was interested in a caribou, and since the fall migration, toward the mainland, was in progress, he and Park left for the marshes to the west, and returned late in the day with a beautiful white-maned animal with impressive antlers.

Next morning I went out with Park for caribou, and we hunted all day in the marsh. We saw hundreds of caribou in all sizes and shapes, except extra large, which we were looking for. The light rain became quite heavy, and the ceilings lowered, so we returned to camp. In late afternoon we hunted in the camp environs, and were surprised to find a couple of graves on a hill top. Each was marked by the remains of a Russian cross made of wood. We wondered what the story of those individuals had been.

Next morning we were again in weather trouble in spades, with a wind of over 40 knots, and heavy rain. By now we knew that we couldn't hunt in that gale, so we put a couple of extra tie downs on the 180, and stayed indoors. Next day the wind was even stronger, so all hands worked on the 180. We hauled her higher on the beach, and put still more lines on. If we got any more wind, we could have a serious problem. Fortunately, the auto engines held, and we were well equipped with tiedowns. Later Bill went out in the gale and shot six ptarmigan. How he could manage was incredible. He said that the birds were "tied to the ground", they simply could not manage the wind when airborne. We had them for supper.

THE MIGRATORY ROUTE

In the morning the wind was down to about 20 knots, and several patches of blue sky were seen. Bill and I still had caribou in mind, and we were running out of time. Park suggested a lake about 50 miles down the peninsula, which was more nearly in line with the migratory route. He suggested landing there, and hunting the surrounding region. It sounded like a good idea, so we took off. Park landed on the unnamed lake, and ran the floats up onto the mud bank, where we secured them with lines tied to shrub roots. With our present wind, she presented no problem. We could now use binoculars, and we saw a great many caribou in this magnificent game highway. The main problem was — we had almost no cover. The marsh grass was about one foot high, and that was it. No shrubs, bushes, alders or the like were in sight. About a third of the marsh area was under water, varying in depth from a few inches to nearly a foot in some spots. The only possible way to stalk an animal was by a belly crawl, and with the water, that was not only unpleasant, it was exhausting.

The animals were slowly feeding in a northeasterly direction, up the peninsula, so that some of the bands would cross our position. We sat down and waited for developments, having no real alternative. While we waited, within less than an hour, a large band from the southwest progressively approached our spot. We hugged the ground and waited until they were within 400 yards and we could inspect their head dress. Bill found a head that he thought would look well on his study wall, and when the range dropped to 300 yards, he touched off a shot. The aim was perfect, and the animal went down in a heap, and remained there. The rest of the band pranced off, in the manner of caribou, as we came up to the carcas, where we dressed it out and carried it to the 180.

It was still early afternoon, and there was time to look over hundreds of caribou in the parade past our

149

location. What a great way to hunt caribou. You don't have to climb a mountain, nor fight your way thru a tangle of alder, or slosh thru muskeg. Just watch a great parade of animals past your observation stand! About 4:00 p.m. a band of five caribou loomed in sight from below. Four of the heads seemed to be exceptional, but we would have to have a closer look. They were feeding very slowly in our direction, but as they came closer it seemed that they were going to pass our position too far to the north. Bill and Park hunched down, and I began a belly crawl with an interception in mind. This turned out to be very unpleasant, for about half of my route was covered with water. I couldn't sling the gun on my back, and the only way to carry it was slung under my belly. At one point I was in nearly a foot of water, and this submerged the stock, action and the lower part of the scope. The caribou moved very slowly, and every time I could get a look at them, I became more excited.

When I had the targets within 300 yards I decided this was it, and I sat up in six inches of water, dried the eyepiece of my scope, and took a careful look. The band had not been alerted, but the caribou with the most beautiful snow white mane did not have the largest antlers. So I took the largest antlers, and when the animal was broadside, I touched off the .300 Weatherby. The animal went down, and never moved. The rest of the band pranced off, and we went over to the caribou. It was by far the best head I had ever seen. When the head was officially measured, months later, it came out as 410 points. It went into the record book, and has been there ever since.

We now had two fine caribou, and the problem of getting back to camp. To make room in the 180 was a problem. We sawed Bill's caribou antlers in two —

they were not a candidate for the record book. That made it possible to stow them in the fuselage. All of the other gear went into the fuselage without problems, except my caribou antlers — they were too big, and we couldn't saw them in two. Park said the only possibility was to carry them tied to the struts. He had done that before, and it did produce some drag, but the ship could fly, if we were not in a hurry to get home. I tied them under the fuselage, between the two pontoons, well above the water line.

We shoved the pontoons off the mud bank, got aboard, and taxied for take-off. There was no doubt the plane was fully loaded, and she certainly didn't leap off the water. But we had plenty of water, and with skillful "rocking" by the pilot, we got on the step, and took off. Common practice is to pull the throttle back after take off, to provide a cruise setting, but I noted that Park elected to retain full power for cruise. That helped to compensate for the extra drag of antlers in the airstream. We landed at the camp "airstrip" in about 30 minutes. There was a distinct feeling on the part of pilot and crew, of having had an excellent day of hunting. Not only excellent, but unique. Hunting this game highway is a great experience. I have even forgotten being half submerged during the stalk. Weather permitting, tomorrow we would head for home.

On the way home I still wondered about the really wicked weather we had experienced during the first week of the hunt. So a few days later I went over to Albany Aviation Weather office, and discussed the matter with them. Then the truth came out. While we were in that mess, I was told, there was a major meterological disturbance in the area between Japan and Alaska, which included a full scale hurricane. We were at the eastern edge of the hurricane system!

CHAPTER V

A FAMILY AFFAIR

We were flying to Post Lake in a DeHaviland-Beaver, in crystal clear weather — a rarity in Alaska — and the view was breathtaking. There was no haze in any quadrant, and the Mt. McKinley massif stood out clearly to the east, and the Alaska Range to the west, and southwest. My two sons, Jim and Dave, were along on this trip, and I could hardly wait to land at base camp and point out some of the sights. The most impressive sight to all of us was the constant presence of game. Caribou and moose could be seen at almost any time of the day. Bands of sheep were seen from base camp frequently, and on special days, grizzly and black bears. Where we lived, at Lake George in the Adirondacks of New York, when we saw big game, which meant white tail deer, it was an event. We wrote to the relatives, and remarked to our friends. At Post Lake big game was a regular feature of the landscape. And the rest of the landscape, foreground and background, was a striking panorama of spruce, muskeg, ponds and lakes, with a backdrop of mountains to the north and to the south.

We had come here by a non-stop flight, from Kennedy to Anchorage, a flight which has not been available in recent years. Jim had been here before, but this was a first trip for Dave, and he was very excited about it. To tell the truth, his hunting experience was almost nil, but when this trip was planned, he went to work with great enthusiasm to learn the necessary skills. We have available a 400 yard rifle range, complete handloading equipment and supplies, and a collection of rifles covering twelve different calibers. He read everything he could get his hands on, and soaked up a great deal of the lore from the great outdoor writers like Jack O'Connor. Perhaps influenced by O'Connor, he elected to take a .270 on the trip. He handloaded quantities of ammunition, tried loads and bullets on the range, and when they seemed right, he worked over the woodchuck fields in the neighborhood to the east. He learned sighting in, and bore sighting until he could reproduce his point-of-aim to about two inches at 100 yards, which is excellent. In a few words, he was well prepared for the trip to Post Lake. Jim had gone thru the same apprenticeship some years earlier, so he was a comparative veteran at sheep hunting.

THE BASE CAMP

We landed at the lake in late afternoon, and went to work getting settled in our tents, and getting our equipment in order. We had one unusual item of equipment. I had located, in a WWII surplus store, a huge pair of naval 18-power binoculars. It was too heavy to carry as baggage, so it had been shipped by express to the Seaairmotive hanger, pending our arrival. It was a beautiful instrument, and with it, on a huge tripod, you could look at a grizzly three miles away, and decide if you liked the silver tips in his pelt. When we were in camp, we spent hours looking at the game highway to the south with the "battleship binoculars".

Next, we became acquainted with our guides and packers. I would work with Earl Stevens, who had guided me for many years. Jim Gartin would be packing for us. Earl & I struck it off well from the beginning, and liked each other's style. Earl was not only an excellent guide, he was a gourmet cook, and his preparation of game food was worth a trip to Alaska. Originally, we had discovered a difference in taste — rare versus well done. But after our first hunt, in response to scientific and esoteric arguments, he had been converted to "rare", and he now prepared sheep steaks that were a delight. Jim would hunt with Larry Keeler, who had guided him before, and they got off well together. Dave would have Joe Delia as guide.

Joe was new to Hal Waugh's guide complement, and he turned out to be a great addition. He was a trapper by trade. In the winter he worked in his home area, in the Skwentna River valley, where he was also homesteading. He was an excellent guide and hunter, and in addition he had a charming sense of humor which frequently kept the party entertained.

Actually, we had arrived at Post Lake a bit before our schedule. We had allowed a couple of days for sight-seeing, but Warren had been so astounded to see the beautiful clear weather that he urged us to fly in, before it rained again, which it does almost constantly in Alaska. The sheep season didn't open for a couple of days, so we had a chance to check our rifle's point-of-aim, by taking a few shots at a 200 yard target.

Maintaining a point-of-aim in Alaskan weather is a daily concern, for the rifle stock is alternately soaking wet and dried out, with sometimes disastrous results. We checked three rifles which were ON when we left home, and found that Dave's rifle was off 2 inches, Jim's was off 8 inches, and mine was off 6 inches. It is not a good idea to test shoot a hunting rifle in a hunting camp each morning. The optical bore sighting equipment which solves this problem was not available at that time. Our only recourse was to visually bore sight. There is a "cross-over" point in every rifle, where the optically straight line thru the scope intersects the curved trajectory line of the bullet, usually about 30 or 40 feet from the muzzle. This point is easily determined by firing a few shots at home; in my rifle it was 35 feet. To bore sight, then, one places the rifle on a rest, prone, removes the bolt and looks thru the bore at a target at 35 feet. If done carefully one can be certain of the point-of-aim to within two inches at 100 yards. That isn't bench-rest accuracy, but it's a great improvement on the alternative, in Alaska weather. I have observed a shift of aim as large as ten inches at 100 yards, after a hard day of climbing in foul weather.

While we were engaged in ballistics, and in short exploratory trips around base camp, our packers were taking supplies into the several spike camps which we would be using soon. We went over to the Post River, and found the water level manageable, and hiked across and down stream for about five miles. We came across a large caribou on a sand bar, apparently fast asleep on his feet. We watched him for some time, and not until we came quite close did he rouse himself and depart, and in the manner of caribou, he wasn't even sure if that was a good idea. On our way back Dave spotted a band of sheep on a river bar, which was quite unusual. They generally prefer to be as high on the mountain as possible. There were five rams and two ewes in the band, all very young. The largest ram had spike horns with two years growth, so maybe they hadn't heard about the timber wolf. If they did, in this situation, it would be a fatal mistake. They were very busy at what must have been a salt lick, which is one of the few things that will lure them from the mountain top. When they saw us, they took off down river and then climbed the steep rock slopes on the east bank of the Post. The sheep season was opening day in two more days, so we would be leaving the next morning for "west" camp. Dave and Joe Delia would go to the camp down the Post, and Jim and Larry Keeler would go to a spike camp already set up to the east, near the Kuskokwim. What fun!

SHEEP SEASON STARTS

We left at about 10:00 in the morning and got into west camp in early afternoon. It was a beautiful area, comprised of a mountain cluster running to 5000 feet, with a high valley and minor peaks in the center. We were at 4000 feet, about 2000 feet above tree line, so we were "in the willows". We had no spruce, so the willow, which is a very poor substitute, was our firewood. Cooking with willow is next to impossible, so we had a small gasoline stove. But willow was our only source of heat for drying out, and drying out, especially the sleeping bags, is a major problem in the Alaska bush.

Camp consisted of two crawl-in tents, and between

them we stretched a sheet of plastic near the fire. It had been raining for two hours before we got to the willow camp, and to see Earl start a fire with wet willow was a joy to behold. The fire even gave off sensible heat, and after some hot tea and food, west camp was not as bad as we thought. It was located at the juncture of two mountain streams, with mossy banks, so that there was no problem in finding our bath house — there it was. In late afternoon we scouted the area, and saw a small band of sheep on a meadow, and a number of isolated sheep higher up — but no rams.

Earl had breakfast going by 5:30 the next morning, and we arose to a very frosty day. Jim Gartin was packing for us; so we went down the valley about two miles, and Earl sent Jim down one valley, and Earl and I took another. We saw over 50 sheep on that first day, with 21 in one band. But big rams were not among the sheep we saw. The largest horns we saw were three-quarter curl. Grizzly signs were everywhere, but we saw no grizzlies. There were many isolated caribou, but none of interest as trophies. The next day we would go to the summit ridge, part of the periphery of our area, and see what was up there.

FINALLY, SOME FULL CURLS

We spent three hours getting on top, where we had good visibility. We checked out numerous bands of sheep, but none of interest, and we stopped for lunch on a high ridge overlooking the Post. I asked Earl not to find a shootable ram an the west slope of the ridge, toward the Post, it was too rough to hunt, but that's what happened. Half way thru the sandwich, Earl grabbed his glasses, and I did the same. There were five pretty good rams down there, and as we watched, four more came in sight. In the lot, there were at least five full curls. That interrupted lunch, and any thought of returning to camp at a comfortable time.

It was raining hard at the time, and it took us some time to work our way over the very rocky slope to a position over the sheep, at a range of 300 yards. There we set up the scope and checked the rams, which had not been alerted. After some examination and much discussion Earl guessed that the best ram would go "above 40 inches." At this point the rain stopped and the deck cleared. Finally, the sun came out.

We crawled thru the rocks and got the range down to 200 yards, and ran out of cover. I touched off the .300 Weatherby, and that anchored the animal. The rest of the sheep started a confused retreat. Their instinct told them to go up, but that's where we were, now in full sight. It took some time to decide to go down — they hated the idea — but they finally did. Earl and I got to the ram at about the same time, and I had a tape measure ready. The "better than 40 inch ram" measured 36 and a half inches. We were facing a fact of sheep hunting — you can estimate, but not measure the curl, until he's down. Pity! The bases of the horns were very massive, but without the horn length he'd never make the book. After that disappointment, I noticed that the horns were widely flared, and equal in length. The animal made a beautiful trophy.

We got the ram caped out by 3:00 p.m. and then faced a difficult task of getting him back to camp. Earl carried the head, cape and one hind quarter. I carried my rifle, binocs and 10x spotting binocs, and all of Earl's gear, including his 357 magnum pistol (when he hunted with me he carried no rifle). It took us two hours to regain the top of the ridge, where we first saw the rams. Our descent into camp was partly very rugged, and partly a lot of fun; we found a series of shale slides for over half of the distance. These slides were particularly good, for we had cased them on our way up, and were sure there were no booby trap drop-offs.

At the end of a weary day nothing matches a carefree descent on an Alakan rock slide. If you have the right slide, you may put your feet together and make a short jump to start the slide, and gain a lovely ride of 20 to 30 feet per jump! Near camp we spotted a grizzly sow and cub, and made a small detour. At camp Jim had a fine bed of willow coals, with some moose steaks sizzling. We declared the following day a day of rest, reorganization and redeployment.

The day started with ram steaks, which gets any day off on the right foot. After that, a bath was indicated, and in the absence of facilities, some improvisation was called for. I will omit the details, but with two crystal clear streams coming together just below our tents, streams with moss-covered banks, one can do no wrong. Of course, the streams did have bits of ice at their margins, but with boiling water on the coals, and some large tomato cans, it was delightful. I couldn't help but remember that, at home, we use 100 gallons of water per day per person.

One of the interesting features of our willow camp, which I hadn't had time to notice before, was the parka squirrel — parka because he makes fine parkas. This rodent is somewhat larger than the eastern gray squirrel, and in camp they had become much too friendly. They — perhaps four in number — overran the entire camp, with a preoccupation for food. They had a simple, direct, approach: bite it, and if possible, eat it. They had some success until they found a piece of sponge rubber in my knapsack. This had the right feel, but not the right flavor. They kept trying and trying, and they might possibly have had an upset stomach the next day. Grizzlies love parka squirrels, and when they get through digging up some of their holes, it looks like a squadron of bulldozers has just gone thru. The next day we would go back down into the spruce, looking for caribou, and in a few days, when the season opened, for grizzlies.

NOW FOR CARIBOU AND GRIZZLY

As usual, it rained all night and into the next day. Our trek was only five miles, but we were heavily loaded, and arrived at the site about 2:00 pm. We were back in the spruce, and were going to enjoy every minute of our stay, or, so we thought. We had a group of three huge trees, at the junction of two streams, and soon had the tents erected with a large fire going. Earl put some big slabs of sheep meat on spits to barbecue, and the delightful aroma and flavor provided a perfect antidote for whatever ailed us. But by then we couldn't remember what it was that ailed us.

About 7:00 p.m., when we were basking in the glow of the campfire, someone appeared at the far end of the valley, running like mad. It was Larry Keeler, and that could only mean that there had been some serious accident at Post Lake. When Larry could talk, he said that Jim had cut his hand with an axe, and that they thought an artery was cut, and there was much loss of blood. Larry had been running over all of the conti-

161

guous valleys since 2:00 p.m., because he had no way of knowing where our camp was. He was really a man of iron. He carried only a .38 cal. pistol, with which he had shot a ptarmigan, after which he, "wasn't worried about anything".

We decided we would take a short rest, and then head back to Post Lake. Earl and Larry set a wicked pace, and I tried to keep up as best I could. We got there in 2 hours 55 minutes. We found that Joe Delia had been able to stop the bleeding, and tape up the rather deep wound at the base of his left thumb. He had taken some achromycin. We were relieved to find things no worse. Jim would undoubtedly not hunt for some time, but we felt he was in no danger.

With matters in fair shape, Joe and Dave left for a new spike camp. They had left a fine ram in base camp, and I measured it to be 162 and a half points, which was just over the B&C limit of 160 at that time. After the horns had dried out they would probably not quite make the book. But it was, in any case a beautiful trophy. According to the story, they had found only four rams in their hunting area. A serious problem showed up the first day in spike camp. The screws in the mount holding the scope on Dave's rifle came loose. He had no tool kit, but he did have a roll of black vinyl tape. He taped the scope on, bore sighted his rifle, and shot the ram. That bore sighting practice had paid off. The vinyl scope mount served well for the rest of the hunt.

I love everything about Alaska except the weather, which continued to be awful. It rained hard all night and into the next day, with much fog. Jim's condition was much improved, and Earl and I left for our new spike camp where we had left Jim Gartin and most of our gear the night before. In late afternoon there was a break in the weather, and a strange light appeared, which we identified as sunlight. We feasted on sheep meat, in quantities which would have caused me to be ill at home. But in camp I was always hungry, and noted that my waist line was going down in spite of the high caloric intake. It was evident that the energy expenditure on the sheep trail is very high indeed. In the late decaying sunlight, we found two rams on the skyline rocks above us to the east. In the spotting binocs one of them could be seen repeatedly rubbing the tips of his beautiful full curls against rocks. Here was a mature ram in the seldom seen process of "brooming" his horns. We watched with fascination.

It had rained and the wind had blown all night, but by daybreak there was some promise of clearing. We left before 7:00 to explore an area to the NW which had been on our agenda for some time. We climbed about three hours, stopping occasionally to scope the neighborhood. We saw quite a number of white spots, which turned out to be sheep, and some black spots which turned out to be a black sow with cubs. Fog and low scud persisted throughout the day, so visibility changed every minute. When we attained the topmost ridge, we set up the spotting binocs for some serious spotting of any area that opened up long enough. We found only one band of ewes. In good weather we might have had a chance, but the curtain was only up for a moment, then it slammed down again. In disgust, we decided that we had had it for the day, and left for "home". We had been eyeing some very attractive rock slides on the way up, and it paid off. We were down in ten minutes, and the delightful euphoria was most satisfying. We built a roaring spruce fire for drying out, and cooked some sheep steaks.

We awoke the next morning to a heavy rain which persisted, with fog, all day. We scratched one day of hunting. Our post mortem later showed that it had rained 20 days of the 21 day hunt. The foul weather continued for the next two days, and we were spruce bound, with no place to go. We then found that, in the expectation of having additional game by now, we had sent too much sheep meat back to base camp with our packer, and our larder was about empty. So, we would have to go back to the Lake the following morning, which happened to be the first day of the grizzly season.

A GRIZZLY, CLOSE UP

Our breakfast consisted of almost nothing. We each had one egg, one tea bag, and a patty that contained traces of rice, apricots, dried potatoes, pancake flour and chocolate pudding. With our great appetites, we gulped it down as if it were food. Our bad weather got worse, with drizzle and fog in the valleys, and moderate snow down to about 4000 feet. Our route back took us over a high ridge, and after we broke camp at 8:30 we were soon up to the snow line where we found two inches on the ground. On the way up, the snow depth increased to about six inches, with fog, snow showers and a 20 knot wind.

We were both carrying heavy packs and other gear, and by 11:00 we were pretty well done in. I began to doubt if I would make the summit, about an hour away. The snow was very heavy, in the air and under-foot, and the wind was from our forward quarter. Our pace became very slow, but we slugged along in the knowledge that there was a top, if we could get there. Near the summit, dragging one foot after the other, we saw some breaks in the overcast. We did get on top just about noon, and sat down to recuperate. We had no lunch, due to the local food shortage, but I found half of a sandwich in my bag, left over from day before yesterday. Earl dug thru his pack and located a quarter pound of brown sugar, that he had overlooked in "breakfast" preparation. These items comprised our "lunch". While we were feeling sorry for ourselves, the weather improved dramatically. The fog dissipated, sun came thru broken clouds, and the air became crystal clear, with spectacular views in all directions.

The worst of our climb was over, and with the stimu-lation of beautiful weather, and "lunch", we contin-ued a traverse of the summit ridge. By 1:30 we were at the SW shoulder of the ridge, and started down to Post Lake, which was now in sight about two miles distant, and 3500 feet below our altitude. One of the thrills of hunting, to me, is the constant gamble that is in progress. Rags-to-riches only takes minutes. We didn't know it then, but here we had had a great turn of nature's roulette wheel. We were about to hit a jack-pot! We had barely started our descent to Post Lake when Earl yelled. "Grizzly"! If we still had aches and pains and hunger, at that point we forgot them. We were then quite puzzled that the folks in camp had not spotted the bear. Constant scanning of the slopes is a required duty of all camp personnel. We could only conclude that the folks in camp were into the beer, and were not paying attention to their binocs. Pity!

The animal was on our return path, but across a deep ravine, at a range of 400 yards. He was slowly feeding up a very rough rocky slope partially covered with blueberries. The bear was in and out of sight, in the tangled topography, and a shot from our present position looked very unpromising. So a conference yielded the following plan: Earl would stay here and try to keep the bear in sight. I would cross the ravine, and shoot the bear. What could be simpler?

When I got to the gully it was very much deeper than expected, and it was 30 minutes before I scrambled up the opposite side. I saw no bear, and Earl signaled that he had also lost sight of the animal. It was possible that he had left the area, but that seemed unlikely, since we had his wind. So I continued to move in the direction the bear was last seen, but slowly, with one eye on Earl. All of a sudden, Earl's signals became frantic, and he jumped up and down. I saw no grizzly, but he had to be directly ahead. So, I sat on a rock, checked my rifle and safety, left the scope on 8x, and waited. In a few minutes, a brown lump showed over a rock, and moments later, the large grizzly stood up directly facing me. At 8x the head filled the entire field of view, and every hair stood out in minute detail. I moved the scope from his head, which would have been the safe shot, to the center of its chest, which would not ruin the mount, and squeezed off a shot. The bear lunged backward, and out of sight. I ran to where I could see the bear. It was down. I tossed a rock — and another rock — but it moved not at all. I slowly approached the animal and touched its eyeball with the muzzle of my rifle. My finger was on the trigger all the while. The boar was dead.

I signaled Earl that everything was okay, which greatly relieved him. When he got across the ravine, later, he said that, in the fore-shortened image on his binocs, it looked like the bear was "about to crawl in your lap". We walked off the distance, and it was 30 paces. There is no doubt that it was much too close for comfort, for bears are known to thrash around a good deal when shot. But the .300 Weatherby is an authentic lethal weapon, and a shot thru the heart is very deadly.

A BASE CAMP REUNION

I was delighted with the grizzly. The animal had a beautiful pelt, with a distinct silver tip. We skinned him out, took two pieces of loin meat, and resumed our descent to camp. Grizzly meat, when the animals are on blueberries, is excellent. When we returned to base camp we found that no one there had heard our shot, or seen the bear, and, they were all sober. Dave and Joe Delia, and their packer, Jerry, had just returned to camp. Shortly thereafter Jim and party got in as well. So the entire crew was at base camp for the first time since the start of the hunt, and adventure stories filled the air.

Dave's big moment came when, at one and the same time, he had in range two of the biggest caribou Joe had ever seen, plus two huge bull moose, plus a large mountain grizzly. He took the grizzly — it required four shots from the .270, but the caribou spooked and left. I have previously related that Dave had taken an excellent ram some days ago, with a vinyl taped rifle scope. What I didn't know until then that shooting the ram had been a special experience.

Their situation was similar to the one Jim had two years ago. They found a beautiful ram, bedded down, facing the hunters, and the problem was — how to shoot him without ruining the mount with blood stained hair. Joe Delia had carefully explained the problem of bloody ram hair. The animal was on a rocky shoulder, with a commanding view in the forward direction. The area was devoid of cover of any kind, and the range was 175 yards. Fortunately there was no wind. After much discussion, Dave suggested a shot close to the ground, and into the brisket. Even a ricochet in that area would have to enter the animal. Joe was very much in doubt that a shot could be put in precisely the right place at that range; anywhere else would ruin the cape. More discussion, and with no alternative, Joe finally agreed.

Dave had spent the previous month at the rifle range, and he was sure of his point of aim at that range. His preparation started with the building of a prone rest for the rifle, using a knapsack, a coat and mittens. He selected a cartridge which had a sharp bullet which had not been battered from recoil in the magazine. Finally, when everything was right, he squeezed off the shot, and a wisp of dust showed at the point of aim. They got the ram, with no damage to the cape. Joe was elated. He told Dave, "You really know how to shoot that rifle. We're going to have a great hunt".

Dave was getting a great kick out of his first big game hunt. He and Joe hit it off great together, and packer Jerry fit in very well, too, so they made a great team. Their day started each morning after listening to Joe's amazing tales until their sides ached. Jerry had a good sense of humor, and he was learning about hunting fast. About half way thru dinner one night, he appeared with some "game". He had gone hunting spruce hens with his 22 cal. pistol (Earl said no more of this, with grizzlies near camp). He missed all of the spruce hens, which is almost impossible, but he shot a bird on the Kuskokwim — and had to wade out waist deep to retrieve it. It was a duck with a head the size of a mallard, and a body the same size. He offered it for the larder, but it was not accepted. It turned out to be a drake ruddy duck.

The next day Earl fleshed out the grizzly pelts and I repaired equipment. In this terrain and weather everything that one wears or carries takes a terrible beating. I was looking at my shoes. They were new, and the finest quality, and after ten days in the bush many seams were opening up, and the soles were coming off at the toes. I found an awl in the camp cache and spent the day sewing them up. I thought they might survive the balance of the hunt. Late in the day Dave and Joe returned with a small caribou that we needed for camp meat. For supper Earl served a stew made from the loin of the bear I shot the day before. It was excellent.

The next day Jim and Larry Keeler left for another try at a ram, and Dave and Joe for a try at caribou and black bear, both out of base camp. Late in the day Dave and Joe returned without game, but Jim was not in evidence, and we had some concern. He was hunting with his arm still in a sling. About 10:00 p.m. we saw a flashlight beam far to the south, and we followed it across the lower slopes there, and into the muskeg. The hunters finally arrived about 12:30.

169

They had a fine ram, but it had been a very long day indeed. After the ram was dressed, the return to camp, first thru snow and fog, and then steady rain, took seven hours. They were out a total of 17 hours, and were exhausted. Jim could only carry his rifle, so Larry and the packer had carried the ram's head, cape and four quarters. To manage these heavy loads in the prevailing weather, in the dark, over very rough terrain, was remarkable. Larry, who had had every possible hunting experience, said that it was the toughest trip he had ever made. The hunters were given a heavy injection of grizzly stew, a shot of rum, and all survived.

WE CAN'T FIND THE BLACKIE

Next morning we had sheep liver for breakfast, and there were no left-overs. Earl and I departed early with a black bear in mind. We went to the South Fork and found a high shoulder overlooking a vast blueberry muskeg. It was raining when we left, and in late morning it changed to snow and fog. When visibility dropped to 200 yards, we decided it was a hopeless case. We found a large spruce, built a fire and had a fine lunch, and then returned to camp. Scratch another day, to weather.

We were en route again early the next day, with some improvement in weather. We again found the high look-out point of the day before from which, today, we could look out. During the morning we saw a lot of game but no black spots which we could count as bears. We had a leisurely lunch, and when I was half asleep, Earl found a black spot that moved. The bear was about a mile away, downstream near the South Fork. Our stalk was a bit too hurried, and when we got near the bear, it spooked. I flopped down for a prone shot just as the bear was going over a ridge, at 300 yards. I squeezed off a shot, and the bear was hit in the only place it could be hit. There was a loud "plop", and the bear did several somersaults, then got up and continued into a dense alder growth. It was down, but not out. We shouldn't have had any trouble finding the bear. But when we got to the spot where the bear was hit, we found a broad trail, well marked by blueberries and blood, leading into an alder patch.

It now seems incredible, but we searched until dark for the dead bear, without finding it. We returned the next morning with three packers and searched until there was no place else to search. It was the first case in my experience where we were sure we had killed an animal, and were unable to retrieve it.

CHAPTER VI

HEAD HUNTING, IN B.C.

The B.C. stands for British Columbia, where we hunted stone sheep with Guide and Outfitter, Lynn Ross, in 1963. I had taken a record book ram from this area in 1961. On the same hunt I saw but failed to connect with a magnificent specimen that certainly was a candidate for a spot near the top of the record book listing. That ram may have been the one taken by Norman Blank in 1962, now in the #2 spot in the book — I will never know. On the chance that the huge ram had close relatives, Bill Aydelotte and I intended to look them over carefully. This was a first sheep hunt for Bill, who was only recently converted to sheep from fly fishing and bird hunting. And from the glint in his eye, I soon felt that sheep were winning out. This was a true 21 day hunt, and as events transpired, we were in serious trouble 21 days later, for on the morning of the 21st day we didn't have any rams. But we didn't give up.

We met Lynn Ross at Ft.St.Johns and he drove us to his ranch near Pink Mountain, B.C., about 150 miles to the north. Elsewhere I have described this beautiful ranch, with its 3000 foot landing strip, and 1000 acres of lovely foothill landscape. We had no time to admire the countryside, however, because Lynn's bush pilot was waiting at the ranch with his Super Cub. The two took off shortly thereafter to join the pack train which had gone in several days previously.

The pilot returned about an hour later and reported that he had left Lynn at a sandbar "landing strip", at the planned location of the base camp. However, they had passed the pack train six miles back in the valley, where camp had been established in the wrong location by mistake. Lynn had a warm jacket, but no matches, so he spent a rather uncomfortable night under a spruce tree. He must have slept, however, because the next morning he found that the pack train had already passed him during the night and set up camp at the intended location. The pilot expected to fly us in that same evening, but weather was deteriorating. He did run me in about half way, where we ran into zero ceiling, and where we did a very tight 180 degree turn in a canyon. It rained all night that evening, and into the morning. There was some improvement by late morning. But when the pilot elected to try again, we encountered the same problem, at the same place, and returned to the ranch again.

AN AVIATION MISHAP

We tried yet again in early afternoon, and this time there was slight visibility under the cloud deck. We squeezed thru, and located the base camp some miles into the canyon. The Super Cub had 24 inch balloon tires, which are practically feather mattresses, and which can absorb a great deal of shock. But when we landed, the plane hit a ridge on the sandbar, fracturing

174

the struts on its right landing gear. The right wing tip was also damaged as the plane skidded to a stop, the fuselage was slightly bent, and one blade of the propeller was bent. Fortunately, no one sustained injuries. So, we had good news and bad news. The worst news was that we were out of transportation, and Bill was back at the ranch.

We propped up the plane, so the engine could be run to power the radios, strung an antenna to a tree, and tried all day to establish radio contact, without luck. As it turned out, our pilot was one-half of a two pilot, two plane charter service. After much mountain flying experience, they had established an emergency procedure. If either pilot was unreported for four hours, the other pilot would fly a rescue mission. On this plan, Mrs. Ross, at the ranch, had phoned the other pilot at 5:00 p.m. So, we would wait. Meanwhile, we had plenty of time to move my gear into the very comfortable base camp. It was located at the juncture of two lovely mountain streams, which were loaded with trout, visible to anyone who cared to look. Lynn had an Indian lad by the name of Fred, who would guide Bill, if, and when, he arrived. In addition, we had two horse wranglers, who took care of the pack train and it's movement. Lynn and Fred alternated as cook, and the food was very good.

After supper, Lynn and I rode down the main stream to scout the area. We saw several caribou on the river, but no sheep. The mountains rose steeply out of the river bottom, and included some impressive peaks. We returned to camp just as our search mission, in the form of a Cessna 172 came into view and circled camp. Our pilot radioed a complete report on the damage situation. The pilot in the Cesnna said he would bring Bill in tomorrow morning, and the replacement parts, in a Super Cub.

FINALLY, WE GO FOR RAMS

The next morning Lynn and I left early, to scout the valley where a record ram had been taken on the "only previous hunt" in this area. If the rams had any sense, they would have been in this beautiful valley, but the only thing we saw at the end of a long day of climbing, was a small band of ewes and lambs. Before leaving, Lynn climbed to the extreme summit, to scope the next valley. That too turned out to be a blank. During the day, we did hear some aircraft operations, and when we got back to camp, the Cub with the broken gear had left.

We now had our full hunting party in base camp for the first time, and we agreed that the selection of suitable rams should proceed promptly. At the moment, however, a more urgent matter required our attention. Fred had some lovely moose steaks on the fire, and we greatly needed to restore a large number of calories that we had burned up during the day. These young moose steaks had a fine texture and flavor, and we soon had our calorie count up to a satisfactory level.

FRED HAS A PROBLEM

It gets dark quite late in this area, so we had time to check our gear, and for camp chores. Fred had a camera problem, and since I had a very complete tool kit, and like to tinker with my own cameras, I took a look at Fred's. Things were not too bad, and we soon had the camera shutter clicking properly. It needed a drop of oil, and in fact, was a bit rusty. At this point Fred noticed that one of the four chrome plated screws holding the shutter together was missing. He said that he was certain that it had been in place, when he sat down on a blanket to check the camera, about an hour before. I suggested that it might still be on the blanket, so we carefully picked up the four corners, and looked

176

In camp during moments of rest. Chapter 6.

A typical river bottom "highway" in B.C. Chapter 6.

Even a minor mis-hap can have serious consequences. Chapter 6.

We were lucky—no one got hurt and the plane was not destroyed. Chapter 6.

Chauncey Guy Suits with horses while taking time out to glass for Stone sheep. Chapter 6.

There was always time for fishing. Chapter 6.

Bill Aydelotte and moose. Chapter 6.

The pack train takes a breather in the Idaho Wilderness area. Although splendidly out-
fitted for an Idaho hunt, we were not as successful as the two lucky sportsmen who
hunted on a shoestring and located their trophies with our tennis shoe. Chapter 7

Chauncey Guy Suits takes a six-point Elk in Idaho. Chapter 7.

Post Lake had been greatly "modernized". Chapter 8.

Chauncey Guy Suits with spotting scope at base camp. Chapter 8.

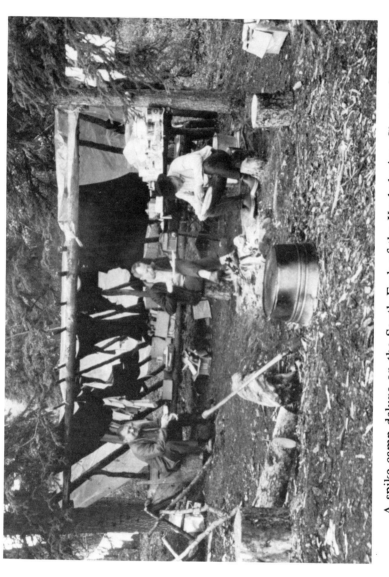

A spike camp deluxe on the South Fork of the Kuskokwim. Chapter 8.

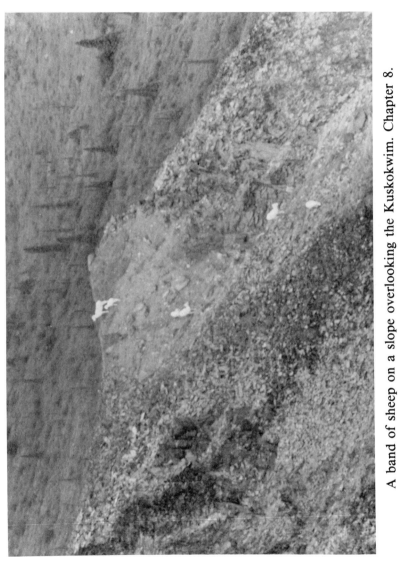

A band of sheep on a slope overlooking the Kuskokwim. Chapter 8.

Left to right: Jimmy Bedford, University of Alaska Professor of Journalism, Bob Stewart, and ram trophy. Chapter 8.

Chauncey Guy Suits and Mr. Big Curl enjoy a panoramic view of the big country.

Mr. Big Curl, big game, big country. Chapter 8.

in the bottom fold, but the screw was not there. I suggested, that since the screw could not fly away by itself, it must be underfoot, but unfortunately out of sight in the rough forest floor. I was challenged by the problem of finding the screw, and quizzed Fred closely. He was absolutely certain that the four screws were in place when he sat down to work on the camera. Therefore, the missing screw must have been underfoot. What to do?

To retrieve the screw, we took a small sauce pan, filled it with rubble from underfoot, and carefully examined the contents, one spoonful at a time. After some time, we had a four foot circle which we judged to be the area of promise, excavated and examined, one spoonful at a time, without result. At this point Fred remembered a piece of fly screen in the cook tent, and screening the rubble thru it went much faster. At this point we were losing daylight, and we crawled into our sleeping bags for the night.

Bill, Lynn and I left early for sheep. Fred remained in camp for chores, including catching some trout for supper. The area we entered was a huge horseshoe shaped ring of peaks and ridges, which included many of the rocky basins that sheep favor. We took the horses up the course of a tumbling mountain stream until it became too steep, and then continued on foot. The day was nearly windless, with scattered cumulous clouds in all quadrants, and the view in every direction was magnificent. In about three hours, we were "on top", and fully engaged in binocular and spotting scope examination of the surrounding territory.

If one could see a sheep at a distance of seven miles, which is the right order of magnitude in clear weather, then the theoretical circle of search, if it were flat land, would include 154 square miles! Of course, our search area was far from flat, which mean't that it included more than 154 square miles. But more important, it included about a million nooks and crannies where sheep could hide. Only a small fraction of this area is visible from the mountain top. Moreover, the slate gray coat of these sheep is near perfect camouflage for the gray rock basins which they inhabit. We spent several hours, including the lunch hour, with binocs and scopes, to no avail.

We did see a lot of goats. There were many small and large bands at various points of the compass. As we started down in late afternoon, we spotted a band in single file, which numbered 36 animals. They were moving into an area in which we intended to move camp tomorrow, so we made a mental note to look up that tribe again. To anticipate my story, we later got into the middle of that band. However, that day we were after sheep, and the goats would have to wait.

We were reluctant to believe that there were no sheep visible in our 154 square mile "circle of search", but we slowly came to that conclusion, and started back to camp. Our burden was eased somewhat by finding a very attractive shale rock slide on the way down. Descending a mountain by rock slide is a memorable experience. On the beautiful slides which almost cover some Alaskan mountains, a descent, after a long climb to the summit, is a lovely way to gain the valley. The B.C. slides which I have seen are not in the same league with the shale slides of the Alaska Range, but they are, nevertheless, a preferred way to get down.

We returned to camp to find a nice bunch of trout on a string at the river bank, and a fresh pile of wood near the cook tent. Fred, however, was not immediately visible. He was still excavating for the camera screw, and we found him at the bottom of his excavation, which was about four feet deep. Sad to relate, the camera screw had not been found, and Fred was at the point of giving it up. This was one of the disappointments of the hunt, but I took satisfaction in witnessing the insatiable persistence of Fred in pursuit of one small screw. In my trade, which is the management of scientific research, that kind of aptitude, is a highly desirable qualification. I thought of offering Fred a job, but then I remembered that he was a bit short on chemistry, physics and mathematics, and deferred. I reminded Fred that the camera worked perfectly well without the screw. This opinion was reinforced by some delightful aromas coming from the cook tent. Lynn was broiling the trout to a lovely brown over the coals. There were a few bones, but we hardly noticed them. I think I remember some Bacardi rum which found its way to the cook tent at about that time, but I can't be sure.

Next day we pulled stakes, and moved camp to a new site, at the foot of "goat mountain". About an hour on our way, I saw a ram on a high shoulder above the creek. The spotting scope showed only three-quarter curl so he was not of interest. This was the only sheep we saw all day. Lynn saw some blue grouse, and shot two of them with his scope sighted pistol, and we had them for lunch. We got to the intended camp site about 5:00 p.m., and the pack train got there a short time later. It took about an hour to get the new camp into a comfortable configuration.

GOATS ARE EVERYWHERE!

It started raining during the night, and continued into the next day. We had quite a bit of trouble with our new ten by ten foot tent, which leaked, and spent the morning trying to cope with the problem. The best solution was some blue sky which appeared around noon. The weather moderated, and after lunch Lynn and I took a ride down the valley, in search of game. We saw no sheep, so we decided to take some time for goat hunting, since they seemed to be everywhere. However, the weather again turned bad and we returned to camp. It again rained hard during the night, and well into the next morning, so that we could not mount an effective hunt during the day. The following morning produced overcast skies and a light drizzle, but we elected to try for goats.

We still had in mind the band of 36 goats we had seen a couple of days earlier. As before, Lynn, Bill and I rode the horses up a narrow ravine with a precipitous mountain stream, until the horses were stopped. We tied them for the day, and continued a steep climb on foot. When we were nearing the summit ridge Lynn reported seven goats at the extreme end of the ridge enclosing the basin. They were about six miles away, and having no better targets, we decided to undertake a stalk. However, the goats were dispersed over a grassy meadow which extended widely between rocky outcroppings. One solitary goat was feeding, directly ahead, on our intended path. We crawled on our tummies thru the fairly tall grass for about 100 yards, and gained cover behind some rocks, without alarming the goat. By then, we were seeing goats on all four quadrants, and we were in the middle of the band. In our post mortem later, we were sure, from the head count available at that time, that this band comprised at least 30 goats! It probably was the band we had seen previously.

After some discussion, Lynn stayed back of the rocks, and Bill and I crawled toward two very fine goats bedded down at a range of about 150 yards. Bill and I took aim, and we agreed to fire at the count of three. We did, and both goats went down, but we did not know that the meadow bordered a cliff, and one of the goats went over. At this point, goats were running in all directions, and in the ensuing melee, Bill and I both took one more goat. This was the wildest goat hunt I expect to experience. Our goat quota was now satisfied, and tomorrow Lynn planned to move camp, still in search of rams.

BUT, WHERE ARE THE RAMS?

We awoke the next morning to a beautiful cloudless sky, and proceeded with the regular routine of pack-to-travel. The operation continued to be one of the wonders of the mountains. I never tired of watching the formation of the diamond hitch, which fastens the pack to the animal's back. It is learned only during the post graduate phase of training for pack train management. When the pack train was ready, Lynn, Bill and I went down the trail in advance, with game in mind. This was a fairly serious consideration, since we were now out of camp meat, and at least needed a moose or a caribou. Lynn again took a few spruce hens with his pistol and that ensured lunch meat for us.

We got to the new camp site well ahead of the train, and Bill was greatly excited by the beautiful trout in the crystal clear waters of the stream nearby. Bill's left knee was giving him some discomfort, an the trout confirmed his intention to stay in camp the next day to give the knee a rest. The new camp was set up on a beautiful spot about an hour's ride from Lynn's principal base camp, which we called "Little Matterhorn", from the towering cliff overhead.

Lynn and I left before daybreak the next morning. We first entered a high basin that the horses could just barely manage. Lynn spotted three rams almost immediately, and in the scope one of them looked very good, until it turned its head to reveal a badly battered left horn tip. The remainder of the basin showed no more sheep, but just before leaving Lynn saw three rams, bedded down, about six miles to the north. He located them by observing a circling eagle, a method that can be highly recommended for sheep which are nearly perfectly camouflaged. The eagle, no doubt, was looking for a small, tender lamb in portable size. The distance was too great to permit a full appraisal of the heads, but, since they looked promising, Lynn decided they were worth a stalk. About three hours later, we were on a ledge overlooking the last known address of those three rams. However, in the manner of big rams, they were gone. We returned to camp and canned rations. We needed fresh meat.

A NEW DEAL, FOR TROUT

Bill and Fred had an interesting day in camp. Bill loves fly fishing, and, by chance he had brought along an Abercrombie & Fitch rod and a bundle of flies. They went to a beautiful pool right next to camp where Bill went to work. Fred in turn, had a somewhat original method of fishing that was unfamiliar to us city folks. He first cut a sapling, and then found a ripe piece of moose meat in the camp dump. His line was a piece of brown hemp cord, with a fishhook large enough for a 30-pound barracuda. Fred's technique was simple and effective. He cut a fairly large chunk of moose meat, put it on the hook, and tossed the rig into the water. When the trout took a bite, Fred jerked the hook and trout up on the beach. As Bill described it, at the end of the fishing a bit later, Bill had seven beautiful trout, and Fred had a "pile". We all had a wonderful trout supper.

The next day turned out to be warm and clear, but at 9:30 I was still in camp. During the night the horses had taken a trip, as horses like to do, and the wranglers were just bringing them in. The horses hated the idea. Much earlier, Fred went out and shot a small bull moose, so we were in steaks again. Lynn and I left camp at 10:30, and returned at 6:00 p.m. after a hard and frustrating day — we had seen two sheep and a moose. After some discussion, Lynn concluded that warm weather was driving the sheep higher than normal. I then recalled that all of the sheep we had seen to date were on the skyline, where it's cool.

We left for the "Big Basin" area where I took a record ram two years earlier. We were now nearing the end of our hunt, and our search was somewhat desperate. To date we had seen very few sheep, and no ram of trophy grade. But in the time remaining, because we had been doing a lot of rock climbing, I felt I could keep up with Lynn, wherever he elected to go. Our entrance to the basin was uneventful, with light rain and much fog, but almost no wind. Three hours after leaving our horses we were on top, without having seen a single sheep. We scouted the summit ridge, Lynn went to east, and I went to the west. We returned to the starting point in about two and one-half hours, with little to report. Lynn saw no sheep, and I saw only seven ewes and lambs.

Meanwhile, some very dark clouds appeared on the north horizon, moving in our direction. When many lightening flashes showed up, we decided hunting was over for the day, and started a hasty exit. We put on our rain gear and made a precipitous ride down the moose trail. About half way to camp we were engulfed by a torrential downpour, with lightening flashes everywhere. The horses were very difficult to control, and our ride down the camp trail was an authentic hair raising experience. We reached camp in a limp condition, that could only be restored by Bacardi rum. Our recovery was hastened by rare one and one-half inch moose steaks, and we lived to see another day.

Still more desperate, with the end of the hunt near, the next day we entered the Robb Lake area, and, in light rain, climbed to the Robb Lake pass. We saw some ewes and lambs. The east face of Mt. Kenny, nearby, included a series of high basins which Lynn said he had never explored, and he now proposed to do so. We made a diagonal ascent over the north slope of the mountain, until we were high enough to look into the basin areas. I found a good lookout point, while Lynn climbed to a higher shoulder. I found several sheep on the skyline too far to the east. Lynn reported later that he had four rams in his spotting scope, but the largest had 34 inch curls, which would not be acceptable. We returned to camp, and licked our wounds. To tell the truth, the next day was the last day of the hunt.

THE LAST LAP, AND A RAM!

Next morning we left camp before dawn, in very unpromising weather. In light rain, the clouds were very low, so that they completely shrouded the nearby peaks. Still within sight of camp, Lynn knocked down a spruce hen, which he put in his pack for our lunch. We headed southwest, for a series of basins we had hunted unsuccessfully some days ago. We saw three rams almost immediately as we entered the first basin, but they all failed the test of the spotting scope. We walked to the extreme western edge of this basin, where it became a saddle, leading to the Ospika River, which is the western boundary of Lynn's assigned hunting territory. To the south, Mt. Knob rises with a moderate grassy slope facing the basin.

As we approached the saddle, a big ram leaped into sight on the south slope. There was no time for measurements, but it was immediately evident that this was the largest ram we had seen on the hunt. Lynn urged me to take him, but the range was at least 300 yards and the ram was running rapidly over the top of Mt. Knob and I deferred. Lynn quickly ran up toward the top, and I was right at his heels. At the top I was completely out of breath, as Lynn explained that the trail went down to the Ospika, and the ram probably would not cross. We got our breath, and then started to check the rocky slope below for the ram. After about 15 minutes, Lynn spotted him, standing on a promontory near the river.

There was no possibility of approaching the animal, so I found a comfortable prone rest, made a range determination thru my scope, by the method I have previously described, and came up with 500 yards. Lynn studied the area, and said he thought it was nearer 400 yards. The difference was very important at this extreme range. We had a stiff breeze at the top of the ridge, but Lynn guessed the ram was completely in the lee. The downward angle was about 20 degrees, which required some under elevation correction. At the end of all of these mental ballistics, I was ready to shoot, and asked Lynn to call the shot. I squeezed off a shot, and a large red area appeared right in the middle of the ram's shoulder. For some moments, the ram never moved, but finally he began to roll down the steep, moderately smooth rock face. This was a very inconvenient spot from which to retrieve the ram, but, on the plus side, he had not rolled into the river.

Lynn said that the only possible way to get at the ram was from the bottom, so we returned to camp, where Lynn took one of the wranglers, and got to the ram some time later. When he returned, we were very glad to see the only full curl ram we had seen on the hunt. The horns measured 33, 34, with twelve and three-quarter inch bases. This was a small set of horns, BUT, he was taken at 11:00 a.m. on the 21st day. He was a very welcome alternative to the big ZERO we were facing earlier in the day.

Bill, Fred and I left next morning in advance of the pack train, for a leisurely trip to the camp on the Ospica. About an hour out we came to a small lake with a large bull moose and two cows, feeding at the lake margin. We had no intention of taking a moose, but the size of this animal caused us to reconsider. He was clearly an exceptional animal, not quite up to the largest bretheren we had seen at Post Lake, but still a huge head. After much debate, Bill decided that he would like to take the animal. The cover was not very good, but he was able to get the range down to 250 yards without difficulty. The moose was slowly moving toward the lake, and in response to six bullets from the 7 mm Weatherby he decided to stop and see what was annoying him. This took several minutes, but he finally found that it was a genuine annoyance, and toppled over. The antlers were very uniform, right, and left, and symetrical, and showed a maximum spread of 57 inches. This interrupted the pack train, when it arrived some time later, but we got to the camp on the Ospica in time for supper.

CHAPTER VII

HUNTING SHEEP, ON A SHOESTRING

Jack Simplot of Boise, Idaho, and I originally met while skiing at Sun Valley. That chance meeting started a long association which led to Zermatt, Davos, St. Moritz and Aspen. We discovered that we also had a mutual interest in hunting, and we had both hunted since youngsters in the areas in which we lived, but had never gone far afield. That was about to happen, and since then we have had some fabulous experiences. Hunting sheep in Idaho comes to mind.

But before we get to that, I should describe our first Idaho hunt, for elk. Jack's pilot flew us separately to a very abbreviated airstrip in the Idaho wilderness area, where our outfitter had previously taken a pack train and supplies. The first evening in camp, elk bugles were heard frequently in all of the surrounding areas. There was no doubt that elk lived here. At the end of 5 days we each had a very fine six point elk. The outfitter did a good job, and the equipment and horses were excellent, and we could think of very little to complain about.

The shot I took at my elk changed Jack's armament for mountain hunting. The tried and true 30-06 had served him well for many years, but we ran into a situation in which it was inadequate. Early on the fifth day of the hunt, after Jack had his elk, we spotted a picture book elk. He was posing on a high promontory overlooking our base camp, about a mile away. He looked very much like a Prudential Insurance advertisement. The guides thought he would probably stay put for some time, so we took off posthaste. We took the horses thru the timber most of the way, and then found that the animal was feeding in a very high brushy area, well out of the timber. On foot, we reduced the range somewhat, but ran out of cover at about 500 yards.

Jack said there was no sense in shooting at that distance. That distance was just what I had been preparing for on my range for a long time, and I said I'd try it. My rifle was the .300 Weatherby, and I had the trajectory nailed down out to 500 yards. My loads were tested to 55,000 pounds per inch square, and with the 150 grain silvertip I measured 3550 feet per second at the muzzle. I put the point of aim on 300 yards and at 500 yards the drop was 21 inches. That is substantial, but with no wind it is manageable. I used a bipod rest, which, in the forest, serves as a bench rest. I squeezed off a shot, and the elk dropped in his tracks. Then and there Jack gave up the 30-06 for mountain hunting. As soon as he got back home he bought a .300 Weatherby, and we have both used these rifles on a great many hunts since then.

RAMS IN IDAHO? WE'D SEE

Many years later, after we had hunted sheep in Alaska and Bristish Columbia, over cocktails one night, we wondered about sheep in Idaho, right in Jack's "backyard". He lived in Boise. It was a fact that there was a small population of Rocky Mountain

Bighorns in Idaho. There was a short open season, and at that time non-resident licenses were available. So, in a spirit of adventure, but with some misgivings, we decided to give it a try. There are not many outfitters in Idaho who have the necessary equipment, and can manage a pack train, but Jack located one.

There was no way of flying in to the intended hunting area, so we went in with the pack train, and at the end of three days we were very comfortably established in a base camp in the high wilderness area. By that time we had a good impression of the outfitter and guides, and the horses and equipment, and were looking forward to an interesting hunt. The main problem was to find a ram. In the country to the north — Canada and Alaska — the sheep live above the timber line, which is in any case much lower than in the U.S. Rockies — 2000 feet in Alaska compared to 8000 feet in Idaho. That's the only way sheep can survive in the presence of the timber wolf. In the U.S. Rockies the wolf has all but disappeared, so the sheep live in the forest, where they are very much more difficult to locate, and they like it that way.

Our hunting routine was very simple and orthodox. We left camp with our horses before daybreak, and spent around ten or twelve hours in the saddle. I knew that western horses could go "anywhere", but Jack took his horse places where even some of our guides feared to follow. In a number of places, they prudently elected to detour. We systematically searched all of the high basins and peak areas we could reach, and at the end of several days it was clear that the sheep population was very thin indeed, or completely invisible. We had seen very few sheep, and nothing approaching a legal ram. On the fifth day, however, we did receive a thrill, of sorts. We came upon a band of 25 sheep, moving in single file from a high basin down into the timber where we were located, and almost directly in our direction. We guessed they would come very close to our position. We had excellent cover, chambered a cartridge, and put our thumbs on the safety. After some time this entire band passed us at a slow walk less than 100 feet away. We could see only two or three at a time so we could only guess what the next animal would be. We had very sweaty hands in anticipation of seeing a trophy ram, but after the last animal had passed, we had not seen a shootable ram. Score: ZERO. This unproductive thrill proved that there were substantial numbers of sheep around, and suggested that a good ram was not necessarily impossible.

THE HORSES TAKE A TRIP, ALONE

The sixth day of the hunt was a long one. We had been in the saddle from 6:30 a.m. until 9:00 p.m., with only a few breaks, and we arrived home exhausted. On the way in we agreed that the next day would be a day of rest and recuperation. But one of the wranglers in camp changed that plan. Jack had arranged to have his pilot fly in that day, just in case we had some problems. It was a good idea, for we had had some serious problems on two previous hunts. We had signals laid on. The pilot circled the camp, as planned, but not as planned, he dropped a tennis shoe which landed in camp. In the toe was a message which said that he had seen a small band of sheep, which included two big rams, on a high grassy meadow SW of camp. He would be back at 7:00 a.m. the next day and circle the area to identify it, IF the sheep were still there. We were very excited by the news.

We were ready to leave camp well before dawn. Two of the wranglers were out to get the horses, and they returned very soon with bad news. All of the horses had been hobbled, front and rear, but they were not tied down. A hobbled horse is suppose to stay put, but smart western ponies have learned that, by hopping, front feet, then back feet, then front feet, they can manage quite well. So, they had taken a trip. They all wear bells, but no bells were heard, so they had gone some distance. At this point most of the camp crew left to find the horses. We thought that they would be back in a minute, and we'd romp up and shoot the rams. As promised, at 7:00 a.m. when we had no horses nor guides, the plane was heard to circle to the southwest several times, and then leave. It was clear that we had a problem.

One guide came back, without horses, and said that he knew the high meadow to the SW, and we'd better run up there as fast as we could. He set a wicked pace as we followed him, first down into a ravine, then up a very long, steep, heavily timbered slope which led to a high summit ridge. He said the meadow was over that ridge on the far side. After about one and a half hours of very hard climbing, when we were near the top, two small rams came down thru the timber at top speed. Something had spooked them. We continued up the slope thru the timber which extended over the top of the ridge, and finally opened into a steep meadow. The meadow seemed to be empty, but we found some movement in the left corner, far below. We hurried down and found a couple of young hunters, dressing out a beautiful full curl ram.

MANNA, FROM HEAVEN

The gentlemen had an interesting story. They said that they were General Electric engineers, working at a project at the Idaho Fall nuclear establishment. They liked to hunt, and they had hunted this area for the last three years, as they explained, "on a shoestring". They had no outfitter nor horses, and they were simply — on foot. Actually, they liked it that way, and the only problem was that, until today, they had not seen a legal ram. But, today, their luck changed. They were coming into the valley about 7:00 a.m. and saw this plane circle overhead several times, then drop a tennis shoe with a note in the toe, which said, "the big rams are at the extreme upper edge of the meadow, just above". They knew the message was not intended for them, but there was no one else in sight anywhere in the valley — they felt very apologetic — so they made a stalk and got one of the rams. We congratulated them on their good fortune and went on our way. Unfortunately, that ram was the only legal ram we saw on the hunt.

The next day was the end of our allocated time, so the pack train started back toward home. When we talked to our pilot several days later he was very distressed by the unfortunate turn of events. When he saw two hunters entering the meadow at the right time, he judged them to be us. He was sure we would be pleased to get the last word on the position of the rams. The wranglers brought the horses back in early afternoon — they had hobbled 15 miles from camp.

CHAPTER VIII

THE PACKERS OF POST LAKE

This was an anniversary hunt — ten years since our first hunt with Hal Waugh, as outfitter, and Earl Stevens as guide. I loved Post Lake, and so many memories have their origin at the place that the hunt had a strong flavor of a sentimental journey. Remains of an ancient cabin on the shore of the lake provided evidence that the lake had an early history. Its modern history started with its development in Post-WWII by Hal Waugh.

I have previously described the lake's location, in the Alaska Range 100 miles west of Mt. McKinley, in a delightful valley between two ranges of low mountains. Sheep live there and caribou, black bears, grizzlies and moose. The fame of Post Lake extends to Europe, and Hal had many clients from Germany and Austria. He said that they were experienced

211

hunters and fine sportsmen. Their interests, however, were quite different from North American hunters. Many were primarily seeking moose, and usually did not hunt sheep at all. Post Lake has a great moose population, and includes some massive heads. My own interest in moose was limited to the lovely rare moose steaks, the way Earl Stevens cooked them. But as trophies — no thanks.

The influx of European hunters to Post Lake brought some changes in camp. Moose hunting was simple, in the sense that the moose were there, and it was easy to find them and shoot them. But a big bull weighs more than 2000 pounds. After you have taken the head and cape, the problem remains, on the ground. Alaska game regulations require that all game meat, except bear, be taken out of the woods. In the worst case, that means, back to Anchorage. In any case, it means that 1500 pounds or more must be transported back to camp. That translates into 25 trips, more or less, for packers with very strong backs. And — they hate it! Walking across the muskeg with 70 pounds on your back is — Ugh!

If a member of a sheep hunting party should playfully shoot a big bull, he would be ostracized by his friends. For that would put a three or four day hold on the hunt, while packers struggled with the meat. I am happy to report that modern technology has come to the aid of the moose hunter, in the form of the "Ranger" vehicle. This charming machine is flown to camp and assembled. Like a small truck, it has four rubber tire wheels, an engine, driver's seat and controls. Unlike a truck, it has two endless belts which run around the wheels. Differential controls provide steering. The belts provide a broad "footprint" which supports the vehicle beautifully over the muskeg which it traverses easily at 15 mph. The Ranger vehicle has taken the pain out of moose hunting at Post Lake. In a few hours it will do what three or four packers would do in two or three days. So, if you want to shoot a moose — okay — no sweat!

My hunting companion on this trip was my neighbor Bob Stewart, of Lake George, N.Y. Earl Stevens guided for me with a young chap named Chip, a packer, and Pappy (Morris) Lee guided for Bob, with Jim Bedford as packer. We came to Alaska by Pan American, and checked in at the Westward hotel. This fine establishment had a restaurant which is famous for many things, especially King crab, which is fresh every day. Before we unpacked any bags, we rushed to the restaurant, and partook of this delightful seafood. Then we tended to business, and such. At the desk there was a note from Hal Waugh, saying that he would be delayed, due to flooding at Fairbanks. We had read about it in the papers. Later we learned that at Hal's home, the water had risen to within one foot of his first floor ceiling. THAT can be a problem! It was the most destructive flood in the history of Fairbanks.

WE FLY TO POST LAKE

We called the air taxi the next morning, and talked to the pilot, who asked us to check out and come to the hanger. Not surprisingly, the weather was terrible, which is common in Alaska. We had steady rain, and a marginal ceiling. But, if the pilot thought it was okay, we'd fly. We were going in a Gruman Widgeon flying boat, identical to the one I was flying at that time, except mine had full IFR instrumentation, which was not needed at Post Lake! Both planes had a gross weight of 5400 pounds, and a useful load of 1500 pounds. These planes, with a 10#/HP specification had beautiful performance, and leaped out of the water on take-off.

We found that there had been changes in base camp in recent years. When we had last seen it, there were three stand-up ten by twelve tents, and several two-man tents, each with a small stove. Now, we found, Hal had erected two guest houses with plywood panels, complete with everything but color TV. We found later that even our spike camp, down the Post, had a three foot high log base, and a tent top. That beats a pup tent any day.

"CAMP COMFORT", ON THE POST

Next morning we left for Post River and our first spike camp. From our previous experience we were well aware of the problems of crossing the icy Post. With all of the improvements in camp, I half expected that Hal might have a suspension bridge across the Post. Unfortunately, no, but Earl had made some improvements. He had found the best possible route over the innumerable tributary steams, and on the two worst branches, with swiftly flowing water 7 feet deep, he had fallen some tall spruces for a crossing. There was 6 inches of water over the "bridge", in the middle, but it was quite manageable, and I crossed without difficulty. The rest of the crossings did not exceed 3 feet in depth. Earl's camp was 4 miles down stream, and it was a spike camp deluxe. At this rate, in another ten years we would have indoor toilets, and a boy could shoot the game while we read the Wall Street Journal, flown in every morning! Ole!

I talked to Earl about the game situation. He said that hunting pressure had been very high, and, until the last two years the heads had been poor. Recently, some good heads had been taken, and some better ones had been seen. For some unknown reason, the caribou population had dropped off drastically. The grizzly population was down with only a couple taken during a season. Moose were on top, but not of interest.

We were now in a position to get serious about the hunt. I should introduce our packer. He was a freshman at the University, where Hal frequently found packers. He was out for track, and he conceived, correctly, that a few weeks of packing in the wilderness might be an excellent way to get his legs in shape for the fall season. However, his hunting experience was zero. He had never hunted, shot a rifle, nor been in the bush. he had heard about bears, though, and felt that some preparation might be an idea. So, he bought an inexpensive bolt action rifle, mounted a scope, found some coffee cans, and started shooting. After some time he was able to hit the coffee can occasionally at 100 yards and with the difference in target size, that should take care of the bear problem. He read all of the outdoor magazines he could find, and something he read there may have saved his life.

We reveled in this luxurious spike camp, and vowed to tell our grandchildren about it. That was in camp. In the bush, things had not changed one bit. There was no easy way to hunt sheep. It still was necessary to climb all of the peaks in sight, where the sheep live.

Our search started next morning before dawn. We entered the steep canyon-like valley immediately west of camp, where we had shot two bears on the earlier trip. The area still looked sheepy, and there were many signs of grizzly, but by early afternoon, we had seen no bears nor sheep.

We searched every side valley, and on many of them Earl went to the summit ridge and scoped the valleys on the other side. When our score was adding up to a big zero, he suddenly saw some white spots many miles off. With the scope on a tripod, and when we were thru counting, we had 21 sheep — all rams! There wasn't a ewe in the lot. There was one band of five that looked impressive, but we were too far away to be sure. Earl was delighted, for this was a better show of rams than he had seen in recent years. Because of the Post River, there had been very little hunting over here. It was almost virgin territory.

Because of the hour, and the fact that there was no way we could get to them in daylight, we returned to camp with the feeling that we at least had a foot in the door. Kit had brought a nice piece of moose meat from base camp, and had a bed of coals ready. Earl's culinary skills were in evidence, and we fared extremely well.

FIVE RAMS ON HIGH

It was noon the next day before we got on top of the ridge again, and weather was poor. It had been raining all morning, and the very low cloud deck was eddying over the ridge, completely obscuring the valley where we had seen the sheep. There was an improving trend in the weather, however, and some time later the clouds broke up and we could see below. There were some high meadows far to the north where the sheep were located, and our count now showed 20 rams. It was now about 2:00 p.m., and time was running out, but we wanted to get a better look at the rams, so we found some beautiful shale slides and went down the north facing slope toward them. After we had covered a couple of miles, the weather, this being Alaska, again went bad, and we were treated to more rain. We gave up for the day, and went down the very precipitous creek bed draining the valley. This was the hardway to descend, but we had no rock slides. We got back to camp soaking wet, and quite exhausted. However, a big fire, some food and rum, and we fully recovered. The next day we would try again. We knew where the sheep were. We just had to get to them.

By mid-morning we were directly under the five rams again. They were on a meadow just below the summit ridge, and they couldn't have picked a more beautiful spot to live. It was a high circular basin, with numerous high meadows in the center and a nearly unbroken circle of high peaks around it. We set up the spotting scope to take a detailed look at the heads. Four of the rams were full curl or better. The largest curl — one and a quarter — looked great, but the bases of this animal were not quite as massive as desired. The second best, and we were not sure it was second, was a full curl with bases that Earl estimated would run 14½ to 15 inches, so we had a difficult choice. We guessed that neither would quite make the record book. But Earl said that they were the best heads he had seen

217

in two years. We had to remember that this was not the Chugach — they don't make Chugach rams at Post Lake. So we concluded we would take one of the rams, which — we weren't sure.

To reach the animals would require a hard climb of at least three hours, under cover. Near the bottom we had an extensive series of steep vertical gullies to climb, and cover was no problem. Near the top we had a massive shoulder for cover, and by early afternoon we were located about three hundred feet above the rams, at a range of about 600 yards. With zero cover remaining, there was no way we could shorten the range, so we decided to out-wait the rams. They were comfortably bedded down and showed no inclination to move. So, we had a sandwich and took a nap. To that point the rams had hardly moved. By mid afternoon, it looked like the rams would win, and we would run out of daylight. In desperation Earl suggested, and I agreed, that he climb to the very summit above the sheep, and make a slow descent.

RAMS, IN THE FRONT YARD

I wondered which of the many departure routes the sheep might take. Most directions of departure would put them out of reach. Usually, when alarmed, sheep prefer to climb, and that was one of the reasons Earl selected the shoulder we were now on, well above the rams. We would soon see! In about a half hour, Earl was out of sight from my position, but possibly in sight of the rams, for the animals got up, and started to stomp around. They were not spooked, but some nervousness was evident. Then, they started to move in my direction, first hesitant, then in a single file up the slope toward the shoulder I occupied. At this point, I was a little nervous.

I checked my gun, safety and scope, then checked them again. The slope was steep, and they were soon out-of-sight below me. My concealment on top was perfect. I was behind a rock cluster, from which I could shoot thru a narrow slot. I don't know how long the suspense lasted, but it felt like an hour. I couldn't tell whether the sheep were continuing toward me, or were headed someplace else. I moved my safety to ON, then OFF, then ON again. More tense moments passed with the issue still in doubt. At this point Earl showed on a crest, high above the sheep, and I interpreted his signal to mean that the sheep were still coming. They were, and soon four rams showed, slowly climbing the slope directly for me. We never did figure out what happened to the fifth ram — he just evaporated. But no matter, he was the little one.

I was still in the dilemma between Mr. Long Curl, and Mr. Big Bases. What a problem! Time was running out, and with a weakness for big curls, and the sheep only 30 yards away, I touched off the 7 mm Weatherby. Mr. Big Curl went down. The other three rams could not see me, and they continued directly up the slope at the same pace, as tho nothing had happened. They came around the rock ledge where I was concealed, and all stopped within 2 yards of my position. I remained motionless, and absolutely fascinated by the super-close up view of these magnificent animals. We stared at each other for many seconds, and then Mr. Big Bases slowly moved off, accompanied by his friends. They were not alarmed, and I was able to observe their every movement as they selected a route over a higher shoulder, and walked out of sight. I don't know whether taking the ram, or seeing one at arm's length was the greater thrill, but, fortunately, I didn't have to make the choice.

I went over to the downed animal, and Earl soon joined me. The head was beautiful. It was now late in the day, and we had quite a bit of work to do. In about an hour, the ram was dressed, caped and quartered. That was the easy part. We now had a precipitous slope to descend, with all the load we could carry, and between us we took the entire animal, including four quarters down to the creek. We temporarily buried the two hind quarters under a pile of heavy rocks. Our packers would pick them up the next day.

PACKER BLUFFS A GRIZZLY

Our packer had made a trip to base camp that day. Otherwise he would have been along for packing chores. As we approached camp from a high ridge, we stopped frequently to rest our weary legs. Looking at the camp below, we had a momentary view of an animal. I guessed it might be a grizzly, but Earl thought it was black bear. There was still some daylight left when we got to camp, and we immediately saw our packer who had brought a huge load of supplies from Post Lake. He was seated, however, and visibly shaken. He talked quite incoherently, and it was some time before he could pull himself together and tell us what had happened. He had been charged by a grizzly!

As he was coming down the trail right into camp, a grizzly cub appeared right on the trail. The boy chambered a cartridge, and before he could do anything else, the sow showed and charged him. He raised his rifle and saw, "a mass of brown fur". At this point the packer remembered some advice he had read in one of his outdoor magazines; "If a grizzly charges, it may only be a threat, and if you yell at the top of your voice, it may stop his charge". He did, and it did! The sow then followed the cub into the bush. He paced the distance off at ten paces. The young man finally stopped shaking, and said that maybe he had been lucky. We couldn't agree with him more.

The hunt had now produced some very exciting moments — rams at two paces — grizzlies at ten paces — but there was more to come. It was time to review our situation and do some planning. We had the ram quota filled, and had seen no caribou worth shooting. We had seen only one grizzly, at great range, and not reachable. So, we planned to go back to Post Lake and regroup. We hated to leave this lovely spike camp, but we came for game. It didn't seem likely that we would find one, but a big caribou was still on our list, and the huge muskeg south of base camp, which was the best place for caribou, deserved some attention. And, we were anxious to learn what Bob Stewart was doing. So, in the morning we crossed the ever treacherous Post again, en route to base camp without any loss of personnel or equipment. We had plenty of "aged" sheep meat in camp, and the tenderloins that night were memorable. There is nothing, wild or domestic, that even approaches "Backstrap of Ram", and under Earl's supervision it was fabulous. For sheep meat, I am running out of superlatives. Pity!

A CLIFF HANGER RAM

We had base camp to ourselves, but before we got

221

organized for caribou, Bob's party returned. They were carrying a fine head, cape and carcass, and were all smiles. When we heard their story, we knew it was true, but it was hard to believe. The hunt had been east of Post Lake, on the mountains overlooking the South Fork of the Kuskokwim. They had seen a great many sheep, including some very acceptable rams, and they finally converged on one that met all specifications. The ram lived in very rough territory, steep and full of crags, and Bob had a difficult stalk to make. He finally had the ram in his scope at 150 yards, and he touched off the shot. Then, like quite a few goats we have known, the ram rolled over a near vertical cliff, fell, and lodged in a crag not far below. To get to the animal from on top seemed hopeless, so they worked their way down to the bottom and tried to climb from there. After several hours, and valiant attempts on many possible routes, they were clearly at a dead-end street. No one could get to the ram. Their packer, Jimmy Bedford, was an experienced rock climber, and even he was baffled.

The party was now in early darkness. They were five hours out of their spike camp and they were facing a night-away-from-home situation. In Alaska that means only one thing — SIWASH. The operation is not unique to Alaska, but it is pursued there with a zest and relish that I have not observed elsewhere. Required is at least one, and preferably three very large spruces, and a supply of firewood. The dense foliage of the Alaska spruce is impervious to rainfall, and under the lower limbs is a circle of comfort that remains completely dry. Preferred is a group of three spruces, closely spaced. With a campfire in the middle one can stay warm and dry overnight. I would like to say that the third requirement — food — is provided by the edible buds on the spruce, but alas, that is not the case. So, the left-overs from lunch, if any, will have to do. That's how Bob's party spent the night.

They went back to work on the ram the next morning, and the task didn't look any easier than the day before. By early afternoon they were out of ideas, and then they noticed that Jimmy Bedford had gone someplace. Without saying a word to anyone he had decided that the last resort was — climb down from the top, which, from the bottom, looked really impossible. After about two hours, Jimmy showed up on the cliff over the ram. He then went down the face of the cliff, one agonizing hand hold after another, until he finally reached the animal. Then he was facing an equally tough problem — how to get the ram down in one piece. Jimmy had a solution to that problem too. He was wearing a heavy woolen sweater, and had a yellow raincoat on his back. He first wrapped the horns with the sweater, and then with the slicker, and tied them in place, and pushed the precious bundle over the cliff. It fell and bounced about 600 feet and arrived at the bottom with the clothing in shreds. But the horns were not broken, and the cape had minor, repairable injuries. Needless to say Jimmy got some lovely new clothing to replace the loss.

Jimmy Bedford, a professor of journalism and photography at the University of Alaska, got very high marks from everyone. He got straight A's, for perseverance, ingenuity and undaunting courage. He had taken the job of packing in sheep country in the hope there might be a story there. There was, and he himself was the hero of the tale. Without his contribution, Bob Stewart might have left his beautiful trophy on a cliff overlooking the Kuskokwim. If we had been inclined to take our packers for granted, we were now keenly aware of the great part they had played in this exciting hunt at Post Lake in the Alaska Range.

The last chapter of this nostalgic return to Post Lake would take place on the morrow, when a Super Widgeon would take us back to Anchorage, en route to New York. It had been entirely unforgettable experience.